How to Be Free

How to Be Free

More Essays on Christian Living

JIM & BESSIE WILSON
and LISA JUST

COMMUNITY CHRISTIAN MINISTRIES
MOSCOW, IDAHO

Community Christian Ministries
P. O. Box 9754, Moscow, Idaho 83843
ccmbooks.org | 208.883.0997

Contents

Introduction

T he title *How to Be Free* is a bit of a misnomer. It is an accommodation to Christians who believe that they are enslaved to particular sins. The truth is that they are not slaves. If you are a Christian, you are already free.

> Since the children have flesh and blood, he too shared in their humanity so that by his death he might break the power of him who holds the power of death—that is, the devil—and *free* those who all their lives were held in slavery by their fear of death. (Heb. 2:14–15)

> Then you will know the truth, and the truth will set you free . . . . So if the Son sets you free, you will be free indeed. (John 8:32, 36)

We are free indeed. "It is for freedom that Christ has set us free. Stand firm, then, and do not let yourselves be burdened again by a yoke of slavery" (Gal. 5:1).

What are we to do with this freedom? "Be ye therefore perfect, *even as your Father which is in heaven is perfect*" (Matt. 5:48, KJV). How can we do that? This verse tells us how—imitate God.

"But love your enemies, do good to them, and lend to them without expecting to get anything back. Then your reward will be great, and you will be sons of the Most High, because he is kind to the ungrateful and wicked. Be merciful, *just as your Father is merciful*" (Luke 6:35–36). Jesus told us to love our enemies. How? Imitate God by being merciful.

> Get rid of all bitterness, rage and anger, brawling and slander, along with every form of malice. Be kind and compassionate to one another, forgiving each other, just as in Christ God forgave you. Be imitators of God, therefore, as dearly loved children. (Eph. 4:31–5:1)

> But just as he who called you is holy, so be holy in all you do. (1 Pet. 1:15)

If unsaved people were commanded to imitate God, that command would make no sense. They are captive to Satan and unable to imitate God. "Those who oppose him he must gently instruct, in the hope that God will grant them repentance leading them to a knowledge of the truth, and that they will come to their senses and escape from the trap of the devil, who has taken them captive to do his will" (2 Tim. 2:25–26).

"And you will know the truth, and the truth will make you free" (John 8:32). We are free, and because of that we have the ability to imitate God.

> . . . because through Christ Jesus the law of the Spirit who gives life has set me free from the law of sin and death. (Rom. 8:2)

> Is not this the kind of fasting I have chosen: to loose the chains of injustice and untie the cords of the yoke, to set the oppressed free and break every yoke? (Isa. 58:6)

CHAPTER 1

How to Be Free from Guilt/ How to Maintain Joy

*I*f you are not a Christian, your feelings of guilt and your lack of joy are tied to many other sins and to a nature that is prone to sin. In order to get rid of all this, you need a new nature, and you need to get rid of your old nature. You cannot do this yourself. It can be done only by God.

Here is your part:

- You need to *want* to be set free from the guilt and judgment for your sins and from the power of sin.
- Know that you are helpless to get yourself free from these sins. Know that being good or not being bad will not set you free, nor will any other means of self-effort.

- Know that God has already accomplished this deliverance for you by sending the Lord Jesus to earth to die for the ungodly. "You see, at just the right time, when we were still powerless, Christ died for the ungodly" (Rom. 5:6).
- Believe that three days after His death for our sins, the Lord Jesus rose from the dead in order to make us righteous. "He was delivered over to death for our sins and was raised to life for our justification" (Rom. 4:25).
- Obey the Holy Spirit, who is now drawing you to turn from your sin and call upon the Lord Jesus, trusting Him, His death, and His resurrection.

That if you confess with your mouth, "Jesus is Lord," and believe in your heart that God raised him from the dead, you will be saved. For it is with your heart that you believe and are justified, and it is with your mouth that you confess and are saved. (Rom. 10:9–10)

Now, brothers, I want to remind you of the gospel I preached to you, which you received and on which you have taken your stand. By this gospel you are saved, if you hold firmly to the word I preached to you. Otherwise, you have believed in vain. For what I received I passed on to you as of first importance: that Christ died for our sins according to the Scriptures, that he was buried, that he was raised on the third day according to the Scriptures, and that he appeared to Peter, and then to the Twelve. (1 Cor. 15:1–5)

Call upon the Lord Jesus. Whei
upon Him, thank Him for bringing yι
for forgiving your sin, and for giving ʏ
life. In the joy of your forgiveness, go and
what God has done for you.

If you are already a Christian and have ι ᴶᵉ joy
you had when you first became a Christian, you can be
delivered from that as well.

> For those God foreknew He also predestined to be
> conformed to the image of His Son. (Rom. 8:29)

> Therefore do not let sin reign in your mortal body,
> that you should obey it in its lusts. (Rom. 6:12, NKJV)

> But now that you have been set free from sin, and
> have become slaves to God, the benefit you reap
> leads to holiness, and the result is eternal life.
> (Rom. 6:22)

These texts tell us that we should be like Jesus Christ.
Jesus did not save us so that we could sin—He saved us
so that we would *not* sin. One of the biggest problems
the average Christian has is how to handle sin in his life.
It seems to be endemic that Christians live with a certain
amount of sin and think that it is normal.

"My dear children, I write this to you so that you
will not sin" (1 John 2:1). The Bible does not command
sin. It commands the opposite. What I am talking

out in this chapter is not the primary solution to sin in the Christian's life, but it is part of God's solution. It is more like rust remover than it is like paint. It doesn't prevent sin, but it does cure it. (We will talk about prevention later.)

There is an old poem I read as a small boy, long before I was a Christian. It was called *The Ambulance Down in the Valley*. It is the story of a certain cliff that dukes and peasants fell over regularly. Everyone was falling off this cliff. The people in the shire needed to find a solution for this problem. They held a meeting, and one of the councilmen said, "What we need is an ambulance. We'll keep an ambulance parked in the valley. Whenever anyone falls off the cliff, the ambulance will be right there."

Everyone was voting for the ambulance when someone objected and said, "No—put a fence at the top of the cliff."

They shouted him down. "What do you mean, a fence at the top of the cliff?! We've interviewed every single person who has fallen off that cliff, and no one has asked for a fence. They always ask for an ambulance. Obviously, the ambulance is what is needed."

God has a fence, and God has an ambulance. This chapter is about the ambulance. Why am I talking about that instead of the fence? Well, when people are already smashed at the bottom, that's what they are interested in. First you need to get yourself fixed up so that you can be interested in a fence.

Blessed is he
  whose transgressions are forgiven,
  whose sins are covered.
Blessed is the man
  whose sin the LORD does not count against him
  and in whose spirit is no deceit.

When I kept silent,
  my bones wasted away
  through my groaning all day long.
For day and night
  your hand was heavy upon me;
my strength was sapped
  as in the heat of summer.

Then I acknowledged my sin to you
  and did not cover up my iniquity.
I said, "I will confess
  my transgressions to the LORD"
and you forgave
  the guilt of my sin. (Ps. 32:1–5)

There are two conditions here. In one case, the person's sins are forgiven; he has confessed his transgressions to the Lord. In the other, he keeps silent. David says his bones wasted away through groaning all day long when he tried that. Have you ever felt like you were just wasting away, groaning all day long, your strength gone? This is because the hand of the Lord is heavy on you for your sin. "For day and night your hand was heavy upon me." Keeping silent is being unwilling to admit sin. Simple admission gets forgiveness.

The subject of Psalm 51 is confession. In verse 13, David says, "Then I will teach transgressors your ways, and sinners will turn back to you." We would like it if being around us caused sinners to turn back to God. We would like to be able to teach transgressors God's ways. But verse 13 started out with "Then . . . " Well, when is that?

Look back at verse 12: "Restore to me the joy of your salvation and grant me a willing spirit, to sustain me." Psalms 32 and 51 both say that the person is blessed whose transgressions are forgiven. The joy of the Lord's salvation is restored *when sins are confessed.*

We would like to think that there are other reasons for losing our joy. "Boy, if you went through the temptation I went through, you would not be joyful, either." But the Scripture says, "Count it all joy when you fall into various [many different kinds of] trials" (James 1:2, NKJV). Trials and temptations are no reason to lose your joy.

"If you were persecuted like I am being persecuted, you would lose your joy." What does the Bible say about that? "Blessed are those who are persecuted for righteousness' sake" (Matt. 5:10, NKJV).

"But I just lost my mother." And the Scripture says, "We do not want you . . . to grieve like the rest of men, who have no hope." (1 Thess. 4:13).

The Scripture also says, "Rejoice in the Lord always. Again I will say, rejoice!" (Phil. 4:4, NKJV).

The normal Christian life is a life of joy. The reason we lose our joy is that we think circumstantially. "If you were in *these* circumstances, you would lose your joy." I'm not saying that there aren't pleasant circumstances and unpleasant circumstances, but when people think that circumstances or environment are reasons for joy, they are not right.

People say, "If I were in Sun Valley skiing, I would be happy," or "If I were married, I'd be happy," or "If I were divorced, I would be happy." When they talk like this, they are saying that their happiness is dependent upon circumstances: good circumstances = happiness, bad circumstances = unhappiness. People who are happy because of their environment and think that that happiness is the joy of the Lord are mistaken.

There is one biblical reason why the joy of the Lord is taken away. "No discipline seems pleasant at the time, but painful. Later on, however, it produces a harvest of righteousness and peace for those who have been trained by it" (Heb. 12:11). God disciplines believers. If you are without discipline, you are not a believer. Hebrews 12:8 says that "you are illegitimate children and not true sons."

When you are disciplined, it is not pleasant. That is the only biblical reason to lose your joy—the discipline of God. When you get disciplined, you say, "Boy, I'm so miserable; I might not be a Christian." Maybe that proves you *are* a Christian. Have you ever known anyone who seems to get away with murder, and it doesn't bother them? Then you step out of line one little fraction and get disciplined fast? It's because the Lord loves you. It is not pleasant. However, if you pay attention to it and respond to the discipline by confessing your sin, you are blessed, and your joy returns.

This is really a six-step process: 1) We sin/disobey. 2) God disciplines us. 3) We lose our joy—God takes it away in order to get our attention so we will 4) confess and repent, 5) be forgiven, and 6) have our joy restored. The graph below illustrates these steps. This is not inspired. The *x* axis, which goes horizontally to the right, is measured in time. The *y* axis, which goes vertically, is measured in joy, love, peace, and the other fruit of the Spirit.

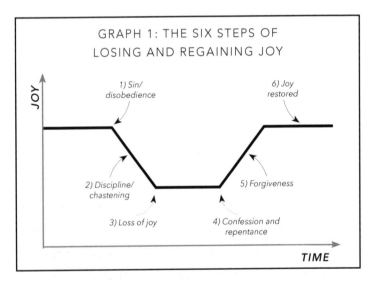

The graphs on the following pages show how these steps played out in my life.

I became a Christian in October 1947 after a Navy football game in Baltimore. I was twenty years old. I was proceeding along the *x* axis at that time, measuring zero joy and peace. I had none. I had the world's substitutes for them, but I did not have the fruit of the Spirit. Right where the cross is, I received Jesus Christ and immediately had love, joy, and peace like I had never had before. The joy continued increasing because of my obedience. My capacity for joy also increased.

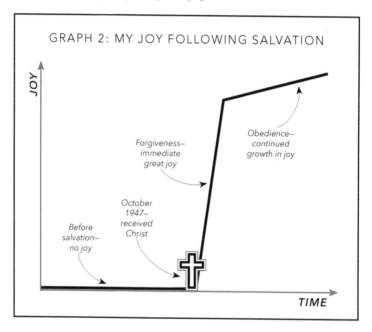

GRAPH 2: MY JOY FOLLOWING SALVATION

I remember the bus ride going back to Annapolis that night, sitting there all by myself. The guys who had led me to the Lord were class of '49, and they had another hour's worth of liberty in Baltimore, so I went back alone. I was so exploding with joy that I made a decision in the first half of the trip to stand on top of Bancroft Hall at the Naval Academy and tell the whole brigade of midshipmen that if Jesus Christ could save me, He could save anybody. However, I had a whole hour to think about that and realized that the Navy would take a dim view of such conduct, send me to the hospital's psych ward for a few days, then ship me home.

"Well, I'll at least tell the people in my company." Then I thought, "No, that's not going to compute. If I tell my roommate that I have just been saved from my sins, he'll say, 'What sins, Wilson? I have been trying to get you to sin all year!'" He already knew I was going to a pre-reveille Bible study seven days a week. He knew I didn't use profanity or slang. "No, that's not going to make sense." I decided that I couldn't tell anybody.

Three weeks went by, and my roommate said, "OK, Wilson, what happened?"

I said, "What do you mean?"

He said, "The last three weeks you have been unbearably pleasant." I have been telling people ever since. It was joy—I had great joy.

The joy was instantaneous when I was converted, and it kept on going up because of my obedience. I am not sure when I started down the staircase of losing my joy.

Graph 3 illustrates what happened when I sinned. As soon as I sinned, I got disciplined, chastised by God. When God disciplines me, He takes away my joy.

Why does He do that? To bring my disobedience to my attention so I will repent and confess. Let's suppose

God did not discipline me. Suppose that every time I sinned I had more joy in the Lord. It is true that where sin increased grace increased all the more (Rom. 5:20). That does not mean we should "go on sinning so that grace may increase" (Rom. 6:1).

No! God takes away my joy so that I will admit my sin in repentance, be forgiven, and have joy again. My descent into less and less joy continued for three years. Yes, I confessed some sins during those years, but my state went gradually downhill.

Well, my joy started going down, but not very steeply all at once. It would go down gradually, then come up a little bit, then go down some more. It went down slowly over the next three years. In the meantime, God was using me in different ways, but my joy was less.

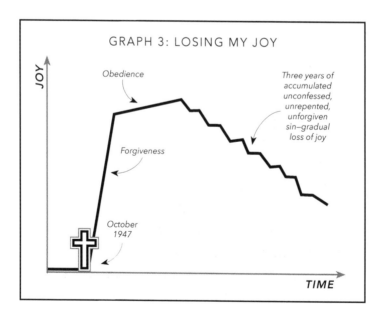

GRAPH 3: LOSING MY JOY

JOY

Obedience

Three years of accumulated unconfessed, unrepented, unforgiven sin–gradual loss of joy

Forgiveness

October 1947

TIME

It was in the Sea of Japan in my stateroom on the *USS Brinkley Bass* (DD887) in March 1951 that I realized what the problem was. It was three years of accumulated, unconfessed sin. I began to confess sin, and as I did, my joy came back up. It was great. It was just like a new birth, except this was not a new birth. When I was born again, I did not confess all of my sins. I couldn't have. I confessed Jesus Christ as Lord. When I confessed Him as Lord, all my sins were forgiven. That was the new birth.

After my restoration in March 1951, I would again disobey, get disciplined, and lose my joy. This time, instead of not confessing, I would confess after a while . . . ten hours, a week, two weeks. So I lived the gap-toothed life shown on the right of graph 4.

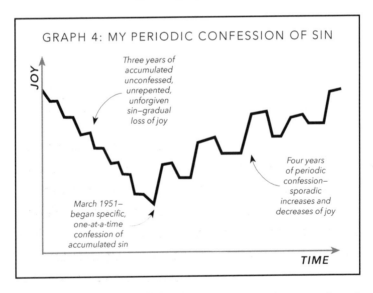

GRAPH 4: MY PERIODIC CONFESSION OF SIN

JOY

Three years of
accumulated
unconfessed,
unrepented,
unforgiven
sin–gradual
loss of joy

March 1951–
began specific,
one-at-a-time
confession of
accumulated sin

Four years
of periodic
confession–
sporadic
increases and
decreases of joy

TIME

I did that for about four years, until 1955. Then I realized that if Jesus Christ could forgive twenty years of sin at one instant as He did when I received Christ, and if He could forgive my three years of accumulated sin in a few hours, and if He could forgive ten hours' worth or two weeks' worth, He could forgive me in one instant. I could sin, lose my joy, confess, and be back in the joy of the Lord in a very short interval of time (see graph 5).

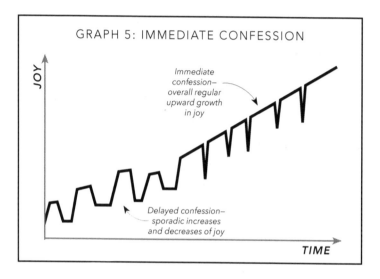

GRAPH 5: IMMEDIATE CONFESSION

Let me give you an illustration. I had learned this truth of keeping short accounts in March 1951, but I did not always live by it. Then in April 1952, I got married. I had all the qualifications of a new husband. It only takes one: Dumb! Some people stay dumb for quite a while. I found out that I could offend my dear bride all kinds of ways by just being thoughtless. I do not think I was ever malicious. I don't think I ever tried to "get to" her. But I managed.

I was dumb, but I was not so dumb that I did not know when I had offended her. I found myself living in a cold house. I could figure out that there was something wrong someplace. I would find out what it was, and when I did, I would confess to God. God would forgive me. It was God I had sinned against when I failed to do what He said: "Husbands, love your wives just as Christ loved the church and gave himself up for her" (Eph. 5:25).

Let me get this across clearly: sin is never social. It is never horizontal. *God* is the one who gives the commands. *God* is the one against whom I sin, and *God* is the one who forgives. When God forgives me, I'm forgiven. The other person may or may not forgive. But if I confess it to God, I am really forgiven. Sin is against God, so I confess to Him.

Only *after* I am forgiven by God do I go and make things right with the other person. So I would get right with God, confess to my wife, and be back in the joy of the Lord.

2 Corinthians 7:10 says, "For godly sorrow produces repentance leading to salvation, not to be regretted; but the sorrow of the world produces death" (NKJV). Notice that there are two kinds of sorrow. There is a sorrow that causes death and a godly sorrow that causes repentance. If you have godly sorrow and you repent, God forgives you, and the sorrow ends. Worldly sorrow says, "You sinned. You should be sorry," day after day after day. People believe it. They carry remorse around until they die.

Then from 1955 I learned and began to practice immediate confession or, if not immediate, close to it. If I had a collision with my wife at 8 a.m., one of us called the other by 10 a.m. If we didn't, it would be one awful day. People would be looking to me for solutions to their problems, and I would be hurting and spiritually dragging. It wasn't worth it.

Get on the phone with God and get on the phone with your wife. If you wait until bedtime to make things right, you have just lost your day. There have been times in these many years that I carried things for a month or two, and I probably knew about my sin at the time and could have confessed it right away.

Sometimes I go for a while before confessing, but generally I confess right away or within a couple of hours. I'm not saying I have not sinned in these years. My family remembers most of them. They could probably tell me when I did. But I have a low tolerance for discipline. I do not like it. As long as I am unrepentant, the discipline stays on me; the hand of the Lord is heavy. I can remove the discipline of the Lord by repenting *now*.

Here are fourteen ways to stay miserable. You can find occurrences of these in the Scripture:

Satan's Lies
- Justify—"It was really right."
- Excuse—"It was really wrong, but . . ."
- Hide.

- Pass the buck.
- Put it off.
- Confess in vague terms.
- Call sins mistakes.
- Say, "I've got too many sins to confess."
- Say, "I can't remember them all."
- Say, "Nobody's perfect" or "I'm only human."
- Say, "I'm going to do it again, so why confess?"
- Be too proud to make restitution.
- Hold on to bitterness.
- Be introspective.

1. Justify—"It was really right"

I am not forgiven, I have no joy, the hand of the Lord stays heavy upon me, and my moisture is turned into the drought of summer, all because I am saying that what I have done is right.

2. Excuse—"It was really wrong, but. . ."

An excuse is the opposite of justifying. Justifying says it was right; an excuse says it was really wrong, *but* . . . If I confessed that what I had done was wrong, period, I would be forgiven. But if I say, "It is really wrong, *but*," and tell God all kinds of reasons why I did it, I do not get forgiven. God does not want the song and dance. He does not want the explanation. When I confess, I am forgiven. When I confess and then say "but . . . ," there is no forgiveness.

3. Hide

Did Adam and Eve hide their sin from God? As long as they were hiding, were they forgiven? No! People still hide. In fact, *cover-up* is a modern-day word. When people cover up, they are hiding, but God still sees the sin, and their joy will not come back until they confess that sin to Him.

4. Pass the buck

We have been doing this for a long time. It doesn't work. Eve said, "The serpent deceived me." That was true, but she was still blaming the serpent. Adam said, "The woman *You* gave me, God, she gave it to me." Whose fault was it *really?* People blame God and then wonder why they are not forgiven.

As long as I am confessing my *wife's* sin, my joy does not come back. Even if she is not in sin, I say, "She is the reason I am in sin." My joy still does not come back, because she is *not* the reason I am in sin. "Well, did she help you along?" Maybe, maybe not, but whatever the case, she is *not* the reason. I am in sin because I chose to sin.

5. Put it off

Procrastinate. We mentioned this already. Suppose my joy level is high, but then I have a collision with my wife at 8 o'clock in the morning. As soon as it is over, I know that I was in the wrong. I know it, but I think,

"This is not the right time to admit it, so I will confess it tonight when I go to bed. No sense letting her know I was wrong now. If I confess it to God now, I will probably have to confess it to her now, so I will just wait and confess it tonight." So what happens to my day? It is awful! Not only do I stay under discipline of the Lord, but I collect more sins during the day because I am in no condition to withstand any temptation that comes my way.

I promised the Lord in the morning that when I confessed my sin that night, I would not justify myself, I would not say I was right, I would not excuse myself, I would not hide it, I would not blame my wife. I would confess it openly and honestly *later*.

So I am going to keep my word. At 11 p.m. I confess all dozen sins. I am back in the joy of the Lord for the eight hours I am asleep. I have perfect fellowship with God. I do the same thing again tomorrow; I put it off till bedtime, confess all of my sins, and have eight more hours of peace with God and joy in the Lord.

Look at graph 6. It's funny, isn't it! I have had lots of people say to me, "Jim, I confess my sins every night before I go to bed," and they do not laugh when they say that because they think for some reason that that was the right thing to do. Yes, it is better than not confessing, but if they had confessed the first sin when it occurred, most of the others would not have happened at all, and they could have gone through the day in joy. Most people don't even confess at night.

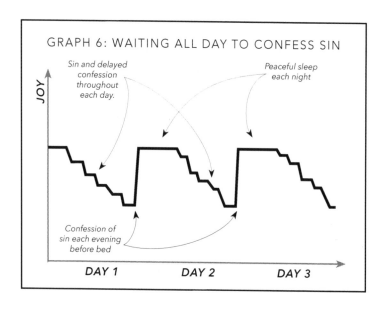

GRAPH 6: WAITING ALL DAY TO CONFESS SIN

Sin and delayed confession throughout each day.

Peaceful sleep each night

JOY

Confession of sin each evening before bed

DAY 1   DAY 2   DAY 3

6. Use vague terms

This is general confession. It is accumulating sins all day, then getting into bed and saying, "Lord, please forgive me for anything I might have done today," and rolling over and going to sleep. The result is you have eight hours of no joy, instead of eight hours of perfect joy.

A woman came up to me once at an Air Force base quite a few years ago and said, "I want to tell you that my husband has been quoting you from ten years ago when you were in Monterey." I was afraid to hear what I supposedly had said in Monterey. But it was this: "You cannot go to bed dirty and expect to wake up clean." That is very true.

If you have a physically dirty, cruddy job, you do not say, "Boy, I can hardly wait to get in between the sheets so I can wake up clean tomorrow morning." A lot of people think, "Well, tomorrow's another day. All of this is history. All this is water over the dam or under the bridge; I'll start clean tomorrow." *No way* will you start clean tomorrow! You will start with what you accumulated yesterday. If you want to wake up clean, you need to go to bed clean.

There is a case where general confession is true and right, but only after the specific sins have been taken care of. General confession may cover things that you did not do that you should have done. Psalm 19:12 says, "Cleanse me from secret faults" (NKJV). But don't call sins secret if they are not. Do not make them secret; do not hide them.

There may be sins that you do not know of that God knows. I think 1 John 1:9 also covers that when it says, "If we confess our sins, He is faithful and just to forgive us our sins" (NKJV). Which sins? The ones we have confessed, "to cleanse us from all unrighteousness." After the confession of the sins, there is a cleansing of all other unrighteousness. This is not repetition. This is the faithfulness of God continuing the work of cleaning.

Be specific when confessing your sins. Why? Because confession is made of three things:

- Knowledge of what you have done
- Admission of what you have done
- Intent to forsake what you have done

When you confess, it means that you know what you have done, you admit it, and you have every intention of renouncing it. That is why it has to be specific.

7. Call sins mistakes

"They were errors in judgment." Do not use euphemisms for sin. It will not get forgiven. In the last few decades, many politicians and television evangelists have gotten into moral trouble. In several cases, they did not say it was moral trouble. They said, "I made a mistake." A mistake is saying that $2 + 2 = 5$. That is not a sin. That is incompetence, not immorality. These people would rather be incompetent than immoral. Unfortunately for them, God does not forgive incompetence. He forgives sin. If we call immorality immorality, it gets forgiven. But if we call it something else, it does not. That is just another form of justification, just another way to say, "I wasn't really at fault."

8. "I've got too many sins to confess"

Over forty years ago, I was talking with a young woman who said, "If I had to confess all of my sins specifically, it would take me ten years." I assured her it would not if she just started confessing. People who say there are too many are just making excuses because they do not want to start. That girl was right with the Lord before the weekend was over.

When my youngest son was fifteen, I was getting ready to make one of my trips to the east coast when I

realized I needed to have a visit with him before I left because things weren't going too well. So he came into my
study, and we sat down. He took the floor. He had seen
me give this talk privately and publicly several times, so
he knew it. He started right in and said, "Dad, if I started
confessing my sins right now and continued for the next
ten years, it would only bring me up to mediocre."

I said, "If I were you, I would get started."

When I called home from my trip, he answered the
phone. I wanted to talk with his mother, but he wanted
to talk with me. I couldn't get him off the phone. He said,
"Dad, I want you to know that my room is spotless."

I said, "Would you please give me an explanation
for that?"

"Well, when you are clean on the inside, it is easy to
be clean on the outside." It did not take him ten years.
He got cleaned up on the inside right away and then
wanted to be clean on the outside, too.

There are never too many sins to confess. The
Scripture says, "But where sin abounded grace abounded much more" (Rom. 5:20 NKJV). You cannot out-sin
the grace of God.

9. "I cannot remember all of my sins"

That is probably true, but the ones you cannot remember are not the ones that are bothering you anyhow,
so start with the ones you *do* remember. As you name
those, your joy will come back up, and very likely your
memory will get better as you get closer to God.

10. "Nobody's perfect" or "I am only human"

These are two ways of saying that sin is inevitable. They are simply excuses.

11. "I'm going to do it again, so why confess?"

If I say, "Lord, just forgive me for everything," I will not be forgiven if I don't have any intention of quitting it. Some people quit confessing because they don't intend to quit sinning. "I will do it again, so why confess?" In other words, they do not renounce their sin, although they know it is sin. "Of course I'm going to do it again." But if you renounce it, it is amazing how things will disappear out of your life.

12. Be too proud to make restitution

> The Lord said to Moses: "If anyone sins and is unfaithful to the Lord by deceiving his neighbor about something entrusted to him or left in his care or stolen, or if he cheats him, or if he finds lost property and lies about it, or if he swears falsely, or if he commits any such sin that people may do—when he thus sins and becomes guilty, he must return what he has stolen or taken by extortion, or what was entrusted to him, or the lost property he found, or whatever it was he swore falsely about. He must make restitution in full, add a fifth of the value to it and give it all to the owner on the day he presents his guilt offering. And as a penalty he must bring to the priest,

that is, to the Lord, his guilt offering, a ram from the flock, one without defect and of the proper value. In this way the priest will make atonement for him before the Lord, and he will be forgiven for any of these things he did that made him guilty." (Lev. 6:1–7)

This quotation from the Old Testament simply says that there are two conditions for forgiveness: 1) sacrifice for sins and 2) taking the money back plus 20 percent. Jesus is the one sacrifice for sins forever. That is God's part. What is our part? Restitution! If we have stolen it, it is not our money. We take it back. See the story of Zacchaeus in Luke 19. Restitution is not works righteousness.[1] It is an essential part of repentance.

"If a man steals an ox or a sheep and slaughters it or sells it, he must pay back five head of cattle for the ox and four sheep for the sheep" (Exod. 22:1). Notice that this restitution is not 20 percent; it is an additional 400 percent for the ox and 300 percent for a sheep.

The Lord said to Moses, "Say to the Israelites: 'When a man or woman wrongs another in any way and so is unfaithful to the Lord, that person is guilty and must confess the sin he has committed. He must make full restitution for his wrong, add one fifth to

---

1. Making restitution does not "earn" us forgiveness. However, if when we repent we do not restore what we stole, we are in effect stealing it again. For more on this subject, read *Repentance & Restitution* at ccmbooks.org.

it and give it all to the person he has wronged. But if that person has no close relative to whom restitution can be made for the wrong, the restitution belongs to the Lord and must be given to the priest, along with the ram with which atonement is made for him.'" (Num. 5:5–8)

If the person or relative cannot be found, restitution goes to the Lord.

13. Bitterness

Get rid of all bitterness, rage and anger, brawling and slander, along with every form of malice. Be kind and compassionate to one another, forgiving each other, just as in Christ God forgave you. (Eph. 4:31–32)

See to it that no one misses the grace of God and that no bitter root grows up to cause trouble and defile many. (Heb. 12:15)

But if you harbor bitter envy and selfish ambition in your hearts, do not boast about it or deny the truth. Such "wisdom" does not come down from heaven but is earthly, unspiritual, of the devil. For where you have envy and selfish ambition, there you find disorder and every evil practice. (James 3:14–16)

Bitterness is simply prolonged resentment. It is difficult to repent of because it focuses us on the other person's sin. Bitterness is our own sin, regardless how wrong the other person is. It makes no sense to stay miserable because someone else is in sin.

14. Introspection

> But only the redeemed will walk there, and those the Lord has rescued will return. They will enter Zion with singing; everlasting joy will crown their heads. Gladness and joy will overtake them, and sorrow and sighing will flee away. (Isa. 35:9b-10)

> Though you have not seen him, you love him; and even though you do not see him now, you believe in him and are filled with an inexpressible and glorious joy. (1 Pet. 1:8)

Introspection is not the same as God's inspection. It is accusatory, and it is a downer. It does not aid in confession. It is a hindrance to it. Introspection needs to be confessed as sin in itself.

If you are not a Christian, confessing individual sins will not work as a solution for being free from guilt. If you are not a believer, you might be in one of these two conditions: 1) your conscience does not seem to work at all; 2) your conscience is oversensitive, and nothing seems to cleanse it.

The solution to both of these is to believe that Jesus Christ is the Son of God, that He created everything that is created, and that He became a man so that He could die and pay the penalty for all sinners.

Christ did not die for good people. He only died for sinners. You have to qualify as a sinner in order to qualify for salvation. The only thing you need to do to get into heaven is to be bad. "You see, at just the right time, when we were still powerless, Christ died for the ungodly" (Rom. 5:6). Are you bad? Then you qualify.

"If you declare with your mouth, 'Jesus is Lord,' and believe in your heart that God raised him from the dead, you will be saved. For it is with your heart that you believe and are justified, and it is with your mouth that you profess your faith and are saved" (Rom. 10:9–10). When you call on the Father in Jesus' name, all of your sins get forgiven. You do not have to confess them individually. Your guilt is gone.

From now on, your conscience will be very sensitive. And now, as a Christian, you can confess sins as they happen. "But if we walk in the light, as he is in the light, we have fellowship with one another, and the blood of Jesus, his Son, purifies us from all sin . . . . If we confess our sins, he is faithful and just and will forgive us our sins and purify us from all unrighteousness" (1 John 1:7, 9).

CHAPTER 2

How to Be Free from Bitterness

Get rid of all bitterness, rage and anger, brawling and slander, along with every form of malice. Be kind and compassionate to one another, forgiving each other, just as in Christ God forgave you. Be imitators of God, therefore, as dearly loved children and live a life of love, just as Christ loved us and gave himself up for us as a fragrant offering and sacrifice to God. (Eph. 4:31–5:2)

In our text, we are instructed to get rid of all bitterness. Before we begin discussing how and why this must be done, it is crucial to realize that the basis for all our actions in this regard must be what Jesus Christ has done for us on the cross. In all our actions, we are to be imitators of God.

In the Old Testament, there was a woman whose name meant Pleasant. Her name was Naomi, and she had moved from Israel to another land with her husband and sons. But her husband had died, and within the next ten years, both of her sons died.

She made some comments to her recently widowed daughters-in-law about it. Ruth 1:13b: "It is more bitter for me than for you, because the LORD's hand has gone out against me!" She was comparing in order to determine who had the right to be more bitter.

And in Ruth 1:20–21: "Don't call me Naomi," she told them. "Call me Mara, because the Almighty has made my life very bitter. I went away full, but the LORD has brought me back empty. Why call me Naomi? The LORD has afflicted me; the Almighty has brought misfortune upon me."

Her bitterness was toward God. It was God who had taken away her husband; it was God who had taken away her sons, and she held it against Him. Five times in these three verses she held God accountable for her bitterness.

There are many people like this today. Not only are they bitter; they enjoy being bitter. They somehow like it, and they feed on it. They wouldn't know what to do if they got rid of it; they wouldn't have a purpose for living. They like being bitter.

We know people like that in the world, and we know people like that in the church. It is easy to recognize when someone is bitter. You can see it in the eyes and in the lines of the face—even if the person is young. You can see it in their mouth; you can see it when they're smiling or laughing. You can hear it in the tone of their voice. You can hear it when they protest that they are not bitter. The bitterness is central, and it pervades everything.

There are bitter people in the Bible besides Naomi. In fact, there are quite a few. For example, Jonah was a bitter man. The Lord said to him, "Do you have a right to be angry about the vine?"

"I do," he said. "I am angry enough to die" (Jonah 4:9).

He thought he had a right to his anger. *I like being angry. God, you are wrong to forgive people. I don't want you to forgive people.*

People enjoy holding things against other people. But our text requires us to remove all bitterness and to maintain a tender heart.

Here's the question: Is it possible to be kind, compassionate, tenderhearted, and yet bitter at the same time? These are all interior attitudes. Tenderheartedness, by definition, involves a tender heart. Bitterness is also on the inside. But it is not possible to have two different, contradictory attitudes on the inside.

Paul says to get rid of all bitterness, and to be kind and compassionate one to another. Therefore, the bitterness must go. But before it can be removed, it is necessary to know what it is—and that it is there.

It is relatively easy to see when other people are bitter. But it's not so easy to see it in ourselves. It is therefore important to have a good understanding of the Bible's definition of the problem.

Let us suppose that a Christian commits a sin. He tells a lie, for instance. When he tells this lie, does he feel guilty, or does he feel bitter? The answer is guilty. When we sin, we feel guilty. It is straightforward. Now suppose that someone told a lie about this same Christian and spread it all over town. What does he feel now—guilt or bitterness?

Guilt is what we feel when we sin, and *bitterness is what we feel when others sin against us.* The very definition of bitterness points to the action of another. If we had committed the offense, we would feel guilty and would know that we had to confess and forsake our sin. We might not confess the sin when we are guilty, but not because we did not know what to do. But what do we do with the guilt of others?

Bitterness is always based upon someone else's sin—whether real or imagined. Consider the imaginary sin first. Many times we can be bitter toward someone for what he said, when in reality he did not say it. We heard a false report, and now we are bitter. We wait for an apology which he cannot offer. Shall we remain in bitterness the rest of our lives because he never says he is sorry for something he did not do?

Incidentally, many bitter people cannot imagine the possibility that they are bitter over imaginary sins. As far as bitterness is concerned, the other person's guilt is always real. For such a person trying to be free from bitterness, it is acceptable for them to assume that the guilt of the other person is real, *so long as they get rid of their own bitterness.*

But what about genuine sin? There are many bitter people who really were mistreated by the offender. So how do we deal with a genuine offense?

Bitterness is based on sin that somehow relates to you. It is not concerned with how big the sin is; it is based upon how close it is. For instance, if some great and gross immorality occurs in Iran, Iraq, El Salvador, or Colombia, what do we do? We read about it, but we will not feel guilty. We read about it, but we will not feel bitter. We might be appalled or amazed, but we do not feel guilty, and we do not feel bitter, even though it was an awful sin, and someone actually committed it. So it does not depend on how great the evil is; *it depends on how close the other person is to me.* Bitterness is related to those people who are close.

Who are likely candidates? The answer is simple: fathers, mothers, brothers, sisters, husbands, wives, children, boyfriends, girlfriends, roommates, immediate superiors, immediate subordinates, co-workers, business partners, and maybe some other relatives—grandparents, uncles, etc. There are even many people who are bitter against God.

We do not get bitter toward evil outside of our own immediate contact. Bitterness is based upon the sin of someone who is close to us and who did something to us. It might be minor. It does not have to be great; *it just has to be close.* Does he pick up his socks? No? Can you get bitter over that? Well, no, but what if he does it five thousand times?

You may think you have a right to be bitter. But the Bible does not grant anyone the right to be bitter. The text says to *get rid of all bitterness.*

"See to it that no one misses the grace of God and that no bitter root grows up to cause trouble and defile many" (Heb. 12:15). Here it describes bitterness as if it were a root. A root is something that is underground and cannot be seen. But there can be visible evidence of its presence, as when sidewalks are lifted.

The fact that you cannot see roots does not mean they are not there. Neither does it mean you will never see them. They drink in nourishment, and they do not stay roots. Eventually they come up.

The fruit that is born bears a direct relation to the root that is producing it. The roots of an apple tree provide us with apples. If there is a bitter root, it will bear bitter fruit.

That is what this verse is saying. Beware lest any root of bitterness spring up, cause trouble, and defile many people, which means to make many people filthy. Have you ever seen bitterness go through a church? Bitterness can go through a congregation like a prairie fire. It can go through the work place or a dormitory. Why is this? Somebody decided to share. He was bitter, and he let the root come to the surface and bear fruit. He shared it, and many people became bitter. The author of Hebrews warns us about this. He says beware of missing the grace of God. When you allow it, bitterness comes up and defiles many people. It makes many people filthy.

What happens to a person if he keeps bitterness on the inside for many years? What happens to him physically? Suppose it is bitterness toward some member of the family. He has not shared it. He has not defiled many people—he has kept it down inside. When he keeps it in for some years, he finally begins to hurt. He goes to the doctor and the doctor says, "You are right; you are sick. But your sickness is not the kind I deal with. I am going to send you to the other kind of doctor."

So he sends him to the psychiatrist, and the psychiatrist agrees. "Yes, you are sick all right. And I know why. You are sick because of twenty years of bitterness toward your father. You have kept it suppressed all these years, and it's rotted out your insides. You have kept this poison within, and this acid on the inside has made you just physically ill. So what I want you to do is to go home and share it with your father. Why keep it in and get sick? Let it out. Get everybody else sick."

So the world has two solutions: Keep the bitterness in and make yourself sick, or let it out and spread the sickness around.

God's solution is to dig up the root. Get rid of it. *But this takes the grace of God.* A man must know the Lord Jesus Christ to be able to do this. He is the source of grace.

Christians should not use the world's solutions for bitterness. When Christians copy the world, they have two poor choices. The Bible says to get rid of all bitterness. You must not keep it in, and you must not share it. Surrender it to the Father, through the Son.

"But if you harbor bitter envy and selfish ambition in your hearts, do not boast about it or deny the truth. Such 'wisdom' does not come down from heaven but is earthly, unspiritual, of the devil. For where you have envy and selfish ambition, there you find disorder and every evil practice" (James 3:14–15).

When I was a young midshipman at the Naval Academy, I thought that the pettiness and jealousy I observed would give way to maturity. I thought the higher you got in rank, the more mature you became, the less this sort of thing occurred. But as I grew older, I found out that the jealousy just got more intense. *Bitterness accumulates.* Unless there's a solution to it, people do not get less bitter with maturity. They get more bitter over the years. It gets worse and worse.

And if you harbor bitter envy, evil practice will result. It does not come from heaven. It is straight from the pit and is of the devil. Every evil practice results from this attitude. As should be obvious, we have a real problem. How do we get rid of bitterness?

Before we can get rid of bitterness, we have to realize that we are bitter. How can we tell if we are bitter? One good rule of thumb is this: *Bitterness remembers details.* You have had thousands of conversations in your life, most of which you have forgotten. But this one took place five years ago, and you remember every single word, his intonation, and every inflection of his voice. You know exactly what happened—which indicates you are bitter.

Someone might object and say that it is also possible to have a good memory of a wonderful conversation. Is this possible? Yes, but not likely. Why? Because memory is helped by *review, review, and more review.* People do not usually mull over the wonderful things as much. But they do go over and over and over the bad things. I have done quite a bit of counseling with people who are in the process of getting divorced. I have known some of them since they were married, at a happier time in their life. But at the time of the divorce, they cannot remember a single happy time. All they can remember is what they have gone over and over. They are bitter.

This doesn't mean there were not happy times. It just means that they have concentrated on how right they were and how wrong the other person was. If someone has a sharp, detailed memory for things which happened years ago when he was a child or a young man or woman, and that memory is at all accusative of anyone, then it is an indication of bitterness. And the solution for bitterness is to get rid of it.

I had a wonderful experience one time in Dallas, Texas. I was speaking on a Saturday night at the home of an old friend. Because I was going to be in Dallas, I wrote notes to several people that I knew in the area, and they showed up at this home.

My host asked me to speak on bitterness, which I did. Afterward, a couple came up to see me. I had known them eight years before in Pullman, Washington. The wife said, "We have been married for eight years. The first year of marriage, I was so bitter toward my mother that I laid it on my husband every single day. Our first year of marriage was just awful because I kept sharing this bitterness toward my mother with my husband."

Then she told me that seven years earlier I had spoken on bitterness, and she had gotten rid of hers. One day, she saw another woman who was really bitter toward her mother. She thought, "I can help that woman. I can share all the common experiences. I went to her to share this, and I couldn't remember any of the details. My detailed memory had gone. All I could tell her was I used to remember things, and I do not remember them anymore." The Lord had really taken care of her bitterness.

Another time, I was teaching a four-week course on marriage. I had put a notice in the paper and did not know who would show up. A woman came who had been referred to the class by a doctor. I can honestly say that I have never seen anyone more bitter in appearance in my life. She had forty years of accumulated bitterness. She got rid of it that night and made an appointment to see me the next day at the bookstore where I worked. She came into the store, and I did not know who she was. *She looked so different.* I had just met her the night before, but she was clean inside now.

What is the problem? Why do we not get rid of bitterness? If I tell a lie, I can confess it and be forgiven. In order to get rid of it, I have to bring it back to my own heart. We need to bring the realization of bitterness back to our own hearts. Instead, the temptation is to look at the offender. Look what *he* did. That is the nature of bitterness. In order to get rid of it, I need to recognize that it is *my* problem before I can confess and forsake it.

You say, "I am not bitter. I just get hurt easily." But the symptoms of getting hurt are very close to the symptoms of resentment. Do you know what instant resentment is? You might say, "It is not bitterness—it is just hurt feelings." But there is a close relationship between being hurt and being resentful. Someone gets hurt, and he gets resentful. There is another very close connection between resentment and bitterness. Resentment turns into a deep bitterness.

Bitterness is just resentment that has been held on to. It has become rancid and rotten. It is kept in, and it gets worse.

The links in the chain continue. There is a connection between bitterness and hatred, and a very clear biblical identification between hatred and murder. What I am saying is that hurt can lead to murder. Some might object that this teaching is too strong. But the strength of it is from the Bible.

What we want to do is make it apparent *how sinful bitterness is*. The bitter person must first recognize that he is bitter, and secondly, that it is a gross evil. Again, the reason people do not deal with this sin is that they think it is the other person's sin. The devil says, "Well, when he quits lying, or he quits doing this or that, or when he says he's sorry, then you will feel better."

But suppose he does not quit? Suppose he never quits? Are you going to be bitter for the rest of your life because someone else insists on being in sin? That does not make any sense at all. You may say, "I will forgive him when he says he is sorry, but not until then. I have a right to my bitterness until then. When he says he is sorry, I will forgive him and everything will be fine." You keep this wall of bitterness up, and one day he comes to you and he says, "I'm sorry." Can you forgive him now? No, because bitterness doesn't forgive. In order to forgive this person when he says he is sorry, you have to be ready before he says he is sorry. And if you are ready to forgive him before he says he is sorry, then it doesn't depend on whether he says he is sorry or not. In other words, you get rid of bitterness unilaterally. It does not matter what the other person does.

Earlier I made the point that bitterness seems to stem from the other person's sin—real or imagined. That is only how it appears. In reality, bitterness is a sin that stands alone. The bitter person decides to be bitter independently of the offender.

You say, "No, he sinned against me, and when he says he is sorry everything will be fine." That is not true. I have known situations where an apology was offered, and the person is still bitter. Suppose the offender is dead and cannot apologize. I know people who are extremely bitter, and the bitterness is toward their parents who died years ago. But the bitterness has not died. Bitterness is the sin of the bitter person alone, unrelated to anyone else.

One time around Christmas, I went to the Walla Walla State Penitentiary to spend the day with the inmates. I spent about six hours there. During the afternoon, I was in maximum security, talking about and teaching evangelism. One fellow asked about reaching the really hard-core criminals. I thought he was really interested in such evangelism and talked to him about it. Then I spent time in minimum security, protective custody, and other places. In the evening, I was back in maximum security, and thought I would talk on the subject of bitterness. I figured there were probably some bitter people there.

The same fellow who had asked about evangelism in the afternoon asked me another question. He said, "How can you get rid of bitterness toward somebody who beat up your three-year-old son unmercifully?"

I told him how, and then I said, "You know, when you get rid of your bitterness you can help this person so that he won't beat up other little kids."

He said, "No, this guy cannot be helped."

I said, "Sure, he can."

"No, no."

"Why not?"

"He is not with us anymore."

This inmate had murdered him. He had murdered him because of what he had done to his three-year-old son—that's why he was in prison. But even though he had killed the man, *he was still bitter.* In other words, expressing his bitterness did not get rid of it. Nor did the death get rid of it.

When someone else says he is sorry, it does not get rid of our bitterness. The only thing that gets rid of it is confession before God because of the Lord Jesus Christ's death and resurrection. *This is the only solution.*

You may say that the person you are bitter toward died many years ago. You did not kill the person like the man in prison. Otherwise, there is no difference; the other person is dead, and you are still bitter.

If the person who died was a believer, he is with the Lord, forgiven and pure. You are bitter toward someone who is rejoicing in heaven because his name is written in the Lamb's book of life.

If the person who died was not a believer, then he is under the judgment of God described in 2 Thessalonians 1:6–8: "God is just: He will pay back trouble to those who trouble you and give relief to you who are troubled, and to us as well. This will happen when the Lord Jesus is revealed from heaven in blazing fire with his powerful angels. He will punish those who do not know God and do not obey the gospel of our Lord Jesus."

"Do not take revenge, my friends, but leave room for God's wrath, for it is written: 'It is mine to avenge; I will repay,' says the Lord" (Rom. 12:19). God is just, and God does the paying.

Even if these people were alive, they could not take care of your bitterness, nor could you by going after them. Being dead, they have been taken care of, either way. That leaves you, alive and bitter, hurting yourself and everyone around you for years. Your bitterness is your sin, regardless of what you think caused it. God will allow you to experience the forgiveness and joy that is yours when you repent and confess your bitterness as a great sin against God. We must not keep it, and we must not share it with others. There is only one thing to do, and that is to confess it as a great and evil sin. We must be as persistent in the confession as necessary.

Once I was speaking at Monterey, California, at the U.S. Naval Postgraduate School. There was a man there who had a great reputation as a Bible teacher. He was a line officer in the Navy, but he had been passed over for the command of a submarine, and he was bitter. I spoke on confession of sin and bitterness, and he was really wiped out. He came to see me and got rid of his bitterness. The next morning, his wife said to me, "I've got a new husband." He had been bitter toward the Navy, but it was his sin, not the Navy's.

Amy Carmichael has a note in her little book *If*: "For a cup brimful of sweet water cannot spill even one drop of bitter water, however suddenly jolted."[2]

---

2. Amy Carmichael, *If* (Fort Washington, PA: Christian Literature Crusade, n.d.) p. 46.

If a cup is full of sweet water and is jolted, what will come out of it? Sweet water. If you give it a harder jolt, what's going to spill? More sweet water. If someone is filled with sweet water and someone else gives him a jolt, what will come out? Sweet water. Jolts do not turn sweet water into bitter water. That is done by something else.

Jolts only bring out of the container what is already in it. If you are filled with sweetness and light and you get jolted, you're going to spill sweetness and light. If you're filled with honey, the honey will come out. If vinegar comes out, what does that prove? It shows what was already in the container. In other words, bitterness is not based upon what the other person did at all. It is the result of what we do and are.

Many years ago, I was working in our bedroom at my desk. My wife Bessie was reading in bed. Whatever I was doing wasn't going well. Bessie said something to me, and I turned around and let her have it. It was something un-Christian. She looked at me in amazement and got up and left the room. I sat there thinking, "She should not have said it. Look what she said. Look, look, look." I did that for around ten minutes. I was bitter toward Bessie, but all she did was jolt the cup. What was in the cup came out.

If I had been filled with sweetness and light, the jolt would not have mattered. I sat there and thought about what she did. I knew better, because I had already learned this truth about bitterness. Still, I thought about her "sin" because there is enjoyment in accusing the other person. Some people do this for years.

I sat there for a while and then got up and went over to my side of the bed, got on my knees, and said, "Lord, I was the only one at fault. It was my bitterness and my sin. I am confessing it, forsaking it, and please forgive me."

I got up off my knees and said, "But look what she said." I got back on my knees.

"God, I'm sorry for what I did. I accept the responsibility. It was my sin, and mine only."

I got up off my knees and said, "God, you and I know who is really at fault." I knelt back down. I stayed on my knees for forty-five minutes until I could get up and not say, "Look what she said."

I do not remember now what Bessie said, and I do not remember what I was doing at the desk. I do not remember the details. The only thing I remember now is getting up. But I also know that if I had not taken care of the bitterness *I would know to this day exactly what she said.* That is the nature of bitterness.

In order to get rid of bitterness, I have to see that it is evil, and that it is my sin and my sin only. I do not get rid of it through the other person saying he is sorry. I do not get rid of it if the other person quits or dies. I do not get rid of it any other way except calling it sin against the holy God, confessing it, and receiving forgiveness.

The difficulty is getting my eyes off the other person's sin. But just the fact that I think it is his problem shows that it is not. If it actually were his problem, and I were filled with sweetness and light, and not bitter, then I would be concerned about him. I could say, "That poor guy! Look what he did. If I did something like that, I would feel awful. He must really feel awful. I think I will go help him." If that is not my response, then I am bitter, and it is my sin, not his.

I believe that this sin is a major hindrance to revival in this country. When Christians start confessing their sins, they will be able to forgive the sins of others.

CHAPTER 3

How to Receive Bitterness (How to Handle Bitterness Against You)

irst, let's talk about prevention. How can we prevent others from being bitter toward us? Here are a few good instructions from Scripture to keep you from stumbling others:

> Now about food sacrificed to idols: We know that we all possess knowledge. Knowledge puffs up, but love builds up. The man who thinks he knows something does not yet know as he ought to know. But the man who loves God is known by God.

So then, about eating food sacrificed to idols: We know that an idol is nothing at all in the world and that there is no God but one. . . .

Be careful, however, that the exercise of your freedom does not become a stumbling block to the weak. For if anyone with a weak conscience sees you who have this knowledge eating in an idol's temple, won't he be emboldened to eat what has been sacrificed to idols? So this weak brother, for whom Christ died, is destroyed by your knowledge. When you sin against your brothers in this way and wound their weak conscience, you sin against Christ. Therefore, if what I eat causes my brother to fall into sin, I will never eat meat again, so that I will not cause him to fall. (1 Cor. 8:1–4, 9–13)

"Everything is permissible"—but not everything is beneficial. "Everything is permissible"—but not everything is constructive. Nobody should seek his own good, but the good of others. . . .

If some unbeliever invites you to a meal and you want to go, eat whatever is put before you without raising questions of conscience. But if anyone says to you, "This has been offered in sacrifice," then do not eat it, both for the sake of the man who told you and for conscience' sake—the other man's conscience, I mean, not yours. For why should my freedom be judged by another's conscience? If I take part in the meal with thankfulness, why am I denounced because of something I thank God for?

So whether you eat or drink or whatever you do, do it all for the glory of God. Do not cause anyone to stumble, whether Jews, Greeks or the church of God—even as I try to please everybody in every way. For I am not seeking my own good but the good of many, so that they may be saved. (1 Cor. 10:23–24, 27–33)

Bless those who persecute you; bless and do not curse. Rejoice with those who rejoice; mourn with those who mourn. Live in harmony with one another. Do not be proud, but be willing to associate with people of low position. Do not be conceited.

Do not repay anyone evil for evil. Be careful to do what is right in the eyes of everybody. If it is possible, as far as it depends on you, live at peace with everyone. Do not take revenge, my friends, but leave room for God's wrath, for it is written: "It is mine to avenge; I will repay," says the Lord. On the contrary: "If your enemy is hungry, feed him; if he is thirsty, give him something to drink. In doing this, you will heap burning coals on his head." Do not be overcome by evil, but overcome evil with good. (Rom. 12:14–21)

What do you do if someone else is already bitter against you?

Among your relatives, friends, and acquaintances, there are three types of people: those whom you are very close with, with no obstructions between you;

those that you think have sinned against you; and those who think you have sinned against them. If someone is bitter toward you, what they hold against you could be an imaginary sin, a misunderstanding, or a sin you are really guilty of.

The Scripture has something to say about this: "Therefore, if you are offering your gift at the altar and there remember that your brother has something against you, leave your gift there in front of the altar. First go and be reconciled to your brother; then come and offer your gift" (Matt. 5:23–24). We don't take gifts to the altar any more, but there are other ways we come to the Lord. The most obvious is the Lord's Supper. This is a special remembrance, and 1 Corinthians 11 tells us to do it properly. "Properly" means that your heart must be clean. Come with your sins already forgiven, so you can observe it in real worship to God.

In Matthew 5, three things stand out: 1) You know that your brother has something against you. 2) You need to be reconciled with your brother. 3) You are not to present your offering to God until reconciliation is accomplished.

How do you be reconciled? First, go to him. If you know what the problem is, and it is something you can fix by confessing to God and to him, do it. If you do not know what the problem is, ask him. If it is a legitimate charge, confess it to God and to him and ask for his forgiveness. If it is a misunderstanding or a rumor that is not true, explain it to him.

If the bitter person thinks that you owe him money, determine whether it is true. If it is, pay him the full amount plus twenty percent.

The LORD said to Moses: "If anyone sins and is unfaithful to the LORD by deceiving his neighbor about something entrusted to him or left in his care or stolen, or if he cheats him, or if he finds lost property and lies about it, or if he swears falsely, or if he commits any such sin that people may do—when he thus sins and becomes guilty, he must return what he has stolen or taken by extortion, or what was entrusted to him, or the lost property he found, or whatever it was he swore falsely about. He must make restitution in full, add a fifth of the value to it and give it all to the owner on the day he presents his guilt offering." (Lev. 6:1–5)

If you do not owe him the money, find out how much he expects from you, *double* the amount, and give it to him. "And if anyone wants to sue you and take your shirt, hand over your coat as well" (Matt. 5:40).

If he has taken offense about something you said or did that was not sin, do not apologize or say you are sorry for it. That is a humanistic solution and will not fix the problem. You would be apologizing for his taking offense. You would be apologizing for his sin. Giving offence is sometimes sin. *Taking offense is always sin.*

If someone is bitter against you, go to him. You don't have the option of not going. This is basic, groundwork Christianity.

"But he won't listen."

How do you know he won't?

"My attitude's so bad, I'll fix it so he won't listen."

Spend time with the Lord before you go.

What about when someone has sinned against you? Matthew 18 addresses this. "If your brother sins, go and point out his fault, just between the two of you. If he listens to you, you have won him over" (Matt. 18:15). If he has something against you, go to him. If you have something against him, go to him. In both cases, you do the going.

When you go to be reconciled with your brother, how do you go? If he has sinned against you, you *may not* go to him with an accusatory attitude or accusatory words. The object of this process is reconciliation. If you go with an accusation, your object obviously is not reconciliation, and I can guarantee he won't listen to you.

The last verse of Matthew 18 says, "This is how my heavenly Father will treat each of you unless you forgive your brother from your heart" (v. 18:35). That is right after the "seventy times seven" passage, and it is the conclusion to the story of the wicked servant who would not forgive his fellow servant's debt and was condemned because of it.

Matthew 18 does not say to forgive your brother if he repents seventy times seven, but if he has *sinned*

against you seventy times seven. Four hundred and
ninety times you go to him with forgiveness in your
heart. You bring his sin to his attention, but your heart
is forgiving. The goal is to get him to repent, and you
cannot do that with a belligerent attitude. You go to
him for *his* sake.

Recently, I was talking to someone in a situation
like this. I asked, "If you did what you think this other
person did, how would you feel?" (I find myself asking
this question fairly often.)

He said, "I'd feel awful."

"Oh! So he must feel awful!" I asked him, "When do
you hurt the most: when someone sins against you, or
when you sin?"

"When I sin."

"This brother sinned against you. He must be hurting a lot. Go to him for his sake, not for your sake."

When you go with forgiveness, it turns out to be for
both your sakes. Go with forgiveness in your *heart*, not
in your mouth. If it's in your heart, it will get in your
mouth, too, but if it's just in your mouth, then it won't
be real.

The times when people have come to me like this
or I've gone to them, it has made all the difference in
the world—we reconciled!

One of the basic teachings in Scripture is being *eager*
to maintain the unity of the saints in the bond of peace.
Some of the reconciling you do may be with non-Chris-
tian friends, but a lot of it is within the church of Jesus

Christ. It may not be within the same church, but be-tween two churches: in fact, that may be the reason they are two churches—because they split over attitudes. People are unwilling to tell the other person he is wrong kindly or admit that they are wrong kindly, humbly. And yet it is *basic* Christianity. If they have something against you, go to them. Reconciliation is primary.

If none of these things seems to work, then the bit-ter person is the one who needs the help. If he is still bitter after you go to him, someone else should minis-ter to him. If you try to help him, he may just get more bitter. Do not get bitter in return. Do not lose your joy because your brother is in sin. Love him, pray for him, and take his accusations with joy.

> Blessed are you when people insult you, persecute you and falsely say all kinds of evil against you because of me. Rejoice and be glad, because great is your reward in heaven, for in the same way they persecuted the prophets who were before you. (Matt. 5:11–12)

> Bless those who persecute you; bless and do not curse. (Rom. 12:14)

> Do not repay anyone evil for evil. Be careful to do what is right in the eyes of everybody. . . . On the contrary: "If your enemy is hungry, feed him; if he is thirsty, give him something to drink." In doing this, you will heap burning coals on his head. (Rom. 12:17, 20)

It is possible that the bitter person is not saved. In that case, he may not be able to forgive you or to get rid of his bitterness. What he needs is the Lord Jesus Christ. What should you do for his salvation?

- Live a godly life that cannot honestly be criticized.
- Love him in such a way that he knows you love him.
- Follow the instructions in 2 Timothy 2:23–26:

> Don't have anything to do with foolish and stupid arguments, because you know they produce quarrels. And the Lord's servant must not quarrel; instead, he must be kind to everyone, able to teach, not resentful. Those who oppose him he must gently instruct, in the hope that God will grant them repentance leading them to a knowledge of the truth, and that they will come to their senses and escape from the trap of the devil, who has taken them captive to do his will.

- Follow the instructions in Acts 26:15–18:

> Then I asked, "Who are you, Lord?"
> "I am Jesus, whom you are persecuting," the Lord replied. "Now get up and stand on your feet. I have appeared to you to appoint you as a servant and as a witness of what you have seen of me and what I will show you. I will rescue you from your own people and from the Gentiles. I am sending you to them to open their eyes and turn them from darkness to light, and from the

power of Satan to God, so that they may receive forgiveness of sins and a place among those who are sanctified by faith in me."

If you follow these instructions, you will no longer be the person that he is bitter toward. You will have become his spiritual parent.

CHAPTER 4
How to Be Free from Depression

There are three kinds of depression: biological, psychological, and spiritual. Depression is not necessarily just a spiritual problem. However, even a biological phenomenon can turn into a spiritual problem. How you feel physically can be a *temptation* to spiritual depression. If you suddenly contract a disease that renders you lethargic or incapacitated, especially for a long period of time, it can make you depressed.

If you anticipate those feelings, the biological causes can be addressed before they lead to depression. Consider the biological cause as a *temptation* to sinful depression. What caused you to feel low may be physical, but if you get down and stay down, that is sin.

There is a command against it: "Rejoice in the Lord always" (Phil. 4:4). Your depression may not be caused by sin (e.g., you might be depressed because you have cancer and are constantly ill and fatigued, not because you have violated one of the Ten Commandments), but the depression itself is still sin.

Another biological temptation happens to women regularly. At a certain time of the month, a woman's menstrual cycle results in a great hormonal temptation to irritability. I learned this fact the slow way. After Bessie and I were married, I began to realize that something made her act erratically at certain times, and it seemed to be periodic. Being a dumb young husband, I was puzzled for a while. Finally, I figured out what it was.

I questioned Bessie about it. "Tell me, is this event predictable?" She said yes. "Then I would like you to let me know several days ahead of time, and I will walk softly. I will be kinder and more considerate than is normally necessary, and I will pray with you that this will not be a temptation that ends in sin." We did that for many years with great success.

Some depression is psychological. Psychological depression is largely based upon relational situations—peer pressure, family pressure, anxiety, etc. These stresses are temptations to depression, but not excuses for it. Recognizing them for what they are at the outset is a good way to prevent them from turning into depression.

Once you are depressed, you can be easily swamped by the feelings that come with depression: "I'm no good, I'm worthless, God can't or won't forgive me, everybody hates me, and they should." Regardless of how it started, when you get into this situation, you are in sin. This is a difficult thing to tell a depressed person, because it is what he wants to hear. "Yeah, you're right. I'm in sin." It feeds his depression. But it is not the kind of sin that he or she thinks it is. The sin of "I think I'll go eat worms" depression is *believing something about the character of God that is not true.* It is the sin of believing lies from the devil about God, about yourself, about everyone. "God can't and won't forgive me" is a *lie.*

If a person is only a little depressed, he can understand this fairly easily. But people can be so completely lost in depression that whatever you say makes no sense. You could say funny things, true things, false things, and they just do not hear you.

One time, a woman came to my noon Bible study at Washington State University. I could see she was not getting much out of the first hour. In the interval before the second hour, she hung around. She was a Christian, and she had come to the study hoping to talk to me. I approached her to say something (I do not remember what), and she just broke down in tears. I had to send the rest of the class home.

I spent an hour with her. I tried to make sense. She was not getting it. I tried to explain, but it did not sink in. I decided to try getting through to her by repetition. So for most of the hour I repeated this one sentence over and over again: *Go home and tell the devil he's a liar.* I yelled and hollered and just kept repeating *Go home and tell the devil he's a liar!* Finally, it got through.

What is depression? *Depression is believing a lie of the devil and not believing the character and the truth of God.* This woman had been in awful depression for months. At church the following Sunday, she gave one of the greatest testimonies I have ever heard. She had gone home and told the devil that he was a liar and that she was not going to believe him anymore. What I told her made a great difference. Depression is believing things that are coming straight from the devil.

When you are depressed, write down every thought you have, whether they are thoughts about yourselves, God, or other people. After you have them all written down, get a concordance and look up references for each of these thoughts that supposedly come from God. You will not find any of them in Scripture. All of them are clearly from the enemy. They are lies. That is why depression is connected with sin, even if it has a biological or psychological source: once you are depressed, you start believing things that are not true.

Another problem with depression is that when a depressed person reads the Scripture, he does not find all the wonderful verses; he finds every one that mentions sinning and going to hell. Instead, look up all the positive promises of God. Write them out for yourself. Paste them on your refrigerator or on your bathroom mirror. Recite them out loud to yourself throughout the day. Saturate yourself in the truth of God's loving thoughts toward you. (If you know someone who is very depressed, you may have to help him do each of these things.)

Sometimes you just have to buckle down and fight your way out of the depression. You may not feel like doing the things that will pull you out, but make yourself do them anyway. Use any method to keep yourself from giving in and agreeing with the thoughts that are going through your head. Use any action to counter those lies from the devil, whether it be willpower, whether it be fighting it out yourself, whether it be calling upon God and believing. *Do not agree with the thoughts you have when you are depressed*, no matter how rational they seem or how convinced you are that they are true. *They are not true*. When you are down, of course you will not be convinced that *this* is true. I have only been depressed a few times in my life, but I remember how hard it is. When you are depressed, you do not want to believe the good things God has for you.

It is amazing that we believe things which are very clearly false and seem to be unable to believe what we know to be true. The reason for this is that this is a spiritual battle, not a rational one. Prayer in the Holy Spirit is the way to break through depression.

The Psalms are a good place to learn more about this. There are imprecatory psalms, joyful psalms, and depressed psalms. Psalms 42 and 43 are two of the depressed Psalms. The Psalmist is down in the dumps, but he shows no desire to stay that way. This is the opposite of "Nobody loves me, everybody hates me, I think I'll go eat worms" depression. The author of Psalm 42 has a great hunger to get out of it:

> As the deer pants for streams of water,
> > so my soul pants for you, O God.
> My soul thirsts for God, for the living God.
> > When can I go and meet with God?
> My tears have been my food
> > day and night,
> while men say to me all day long,
> > "Where is your God?"
> These things I remember
> > as I pour out my soul:
> how I used to go with the multitude,
> > leading the procession to the house of God,
> with shouts of joy and thanksgiving
> > among the festive throng.

> Why are you downcast, O my soul?
> > Why so disturbed within me?
> *Put your hope in God,*
> > *for I will yet praise him,*
> > *my Savior and my God.*

> My soul is downcast within me;
> > therefore I will remember you

from the land of the Jordan,
   the heights of Hermon—from Mount Mizar.
Deep calls to deep
   in the roar of your waterfalls;
   all your waves and breakers
have swept over me.

By day the LORD directs his love,
   at night his song is with me—
   a prayer to the God of my life. (Ps. 42:1–8)

The Psalmist sees three things that will help him out of his depression. The first is his longing for the Lord: "My soul thirsts for God, for the living God."

The second is remembering the time when he was joyful: "These things I remember as I pour out my soul, how I used to go with the multitude, leading the procession to the house of God." He cannot comprehend singing now, but he remembers when he did sing. Remember when you were in victory and look to the future. "For I will *yet* praise him, *my Savior and my God*." The Psalmist is down now, but he knows that he will praise God in the future.

This is his third help. He has hope in God. *Hope* is the main way out of depression. Emily Dickinson wrote,

"Hope" is the thing with feathers—
That perches in the soul—
And sings the tune without the words—
And never stops—at all—

If you are depressed, long for God, remember what He has done for you in the past, and in faith anticipate that again in the future. This is the pattern of the rest of Psalm 42.

> I say to God my Rock,
>> "Why have you forgotten me?
> Why must I go about mourning,
>> oppressed by the enemy?"
> My bones suffer mortal agony
>> as my foes taunt me,
> saying to me all day long,
>> "Where is your God?"
>
> Why are you downcast, O my soul?
>> Why so disturbed within me?
> *Put your hope in God,*
>> *for I will yet praise him,*
>> *my Savior and my God.* (Ps. 42:9–11)

The psalmist knows that God is present, but he does not feel Him there. In times like this, it is tempting to believe the devil's lie that God isn't there. It is a conflict between what the psalmist *knows* to be true and what he *feels* at the moment. The subjective "truth" says, "Why have you forgotten me?" But he has the objective truth that God is his rock, and it is that truth that will pull him up.

There are different reasons for the depression that is recorded in the Psalms, but within each Psalm there is always an answer to that depression. If anyone says to you, "God has forsaken me. He must have left me, because I don't feel Him," he is saying the same thing as Psalm 42. But firm hope in a sure thing will get him out of depression. When David got depressed, he preached to himself: "Put your hope in God, for I will yet praise him, my Savior and my God." If you are depressed, keep pointing yourself back to *the love of God for you*, regardless of how you feel. Try to create a thirst, a longing for God. Stir yourself up to remember the time when you did rejoice in the Lord and remind yourself that you are going to rejoice again.

Read through the Scriptures and search for all the verses on God's love and kindness. When you find one, ask yourself if it is true or false. Read the verse out loud to yourself and make yourself answer *true* out loud. Thank God out loud that it is true. That will help you get it into your heart. Here is one to get you started: "*For the Father Himself loves you*, because you have loved Me, and have believed that I came forth from God" (John 16:27, NKJV).

One thing that often accompanies (and occasionally causes) depression is guilt. Some secular psychologists teach that guilt is wrong because it brings you down, so you should not feel guilty. Of course, because a person who is guilty is not rejoicing in the Lord, he does need to get rid of the guilt. Because they do not have a real solution for real guilt, non-Christians will try to teach that the guilt *itself* is wrong, rather than acknowledging that the guilt is a *thermometer* of wrong. They teach you to accept your lying as normal, to accept your adultery as all right, so that you do not feel guilty, because the guilt is killing you. The secular psychologist's solution is to accept yourself as you are, to say that evil is good.

You *do* need to get rid of the guilt, but that is the wrong way to do it. Scripture says no to it. Real guilt is caused by a violation of the holiness of God. Only the death and resurrection of Jesus Christ can take care of that guilt when we believe in Him and confess our sin.

"Godly sorrow brings repentance that leads to salvation and leaves no regret, but worldly sorrow brings death" (2 Cor. 7:10). Godly sorrow causes repentance; the sorrow of this world causes death. But sorrow and guilt are often related. A person can be sorry about something that is wrong and not repent of it, feeling that there is some sort of virtue in feeling sorry. He thinks that if he feels guilty long enough, he will have paid for his sin. This is using penance in place of repentance, and it is wrong. Godly sorrow causes *repentance*, and when repentance takes place, the sorrow and the guilt are taken away.

When you are dealing with guilt or depression, remember the greatness of God and His consistency and steadfastness. In my unconverted days, I was depressed much of the time. I was converted under the preaching of Psalm 40: "I waited patiently for the Lord; he turned to me and heard my cry. He lifted me out of the slimy pit, out of the mud and mire; he set my feet on a rock and gave me a firm place to stand" (vv. 1–2).

Depression is a slimy, miry pit. This is my salvation: "He put a new song in my mouth, a hymn of praise to our God" (Ps. 40:3a).

CHAPTER 5

How to Be Free from False Guilt

*R*eal guilt is taken care of in the cross. There is one condition for the Christian to be forgiven, and that is that he admits his sin before a holy God.

False guilt does not come from God. It is laid on us by the enemy. It concerns things that are not wrong, but that the enemy tells us *are* wrong. When we confess them to God, God doesn't forgive them, because they're not sin. The enemy doesn't forgive them, because he doesn't forgive anything. So we walk around with a continual shadow of guilt.

False guilt comes from holding yourself to man's standards instead of to God's. It is a corollary to legalism. Most people have experienced false guilt at some point. The ones who give it to you the most are those closest to you—yourself, your parents, your husband, wife, roommate, boyfriend, or girlfriend—because you pay attention to their standards.

What is the difference? If you bend the rules at work (for example, rationalizing that because you are a good worker it is OK to take an extra hour off), that is wrong unless you have permission from the boss, and what you end up feeling is real guilt. False guilt occurs when you set higher standards for yourself than the Bible does. Suppose you decide that something has to be done by the first of the month. This is not something your boss has determined; you just set the deadline for yourself. For whatever reason, you do not get to it until the second of the month. You feel guilty because you violated your own stupid rule. It was not a moral rule; it was not God's rule. It was man's rule (and not even some other man's, but your own). Perfectionists do this all the time. They set up false standards, fail to meet them, and feel guilty. This is false guilt.

Some people even feel guilty for others who are not meeting the standards they have set themselves. They feel guilty for *you*, even though your "failure" has nothing to do with them. For example, an acquaintance of mine had a habit of writing in his Bible. One of his friends could not see how writing in God's Holy Word was right and told him he should be ashamed of himself. He did not intend to condemn his friend at all; he simply felt awful for him because he was writing in the margins in his Bible.

Churches can also impose extrabiblical rules on their congregation. This kind of legalism is not such an open-and-shut issue. The Bible speaks of *voluntary* abstinence from certain things (e.g., eating meat, drinking alcohol). If you want to follow these kinds of rules, that is fine, but you should *not* feel guilty if you do not follow them. That is the difference between deciding to follow a set of extrabiblical rules yourself and trying to impose those same rules on others. As Christians, we are allowed to follow any extra set of rules we want to as long as they do not violate Scripture, but we should not feel guilty for failing to follow them since they are not rules that *God* set for us.

Perfectionists' biggest problem is often with people who are not as strict about time, order, and cleanliness as they are. These things are so important to the perfectionist that he has a hard time comprehending that the person who "fails" in them is not in sin. He can describe their failure so that it begins to look immoral: extenuating circumstances that will result from you not cleaning your room, ramifications to the witness of the church, etc. He can make it sound like a terribly serious matter that you did not comb your hair this morning.

Conversely, Christians who are not perfectionists need to be careful not to stumble their perfectionist brothers. Leaving the newspaper on the floor is not immoral. But suppose leaving your newspaper on the floor frustrates your roommate, who thinks it *is* immoral. In that case, you probably ought to pick up the paper for the sake of his conscience. He is the weaker brother from Romans 14:

> Accept him whose faith is weak, without passing judgment on disputable matters. One man's faith allows him to eat everything, but another man, whose faith is weak, eats only vegetables. The man who eats everything must not look down on him who does not, and the man who does not eat everything must not condemn the man who does, for God has accepted him. Who are you to judge someone else's servant? To his own master he stands or falls. And he will stand, for the Lord is able to make him stand . . . .
>
> Therefore let us stop passing judgment on one another. Instead, make up your mind not to put any stumbling block or obstacle in your brother's way. As one who is in the Lord Jesus, I am fully convinced that no food is unclean in itself. But if anyone regards something as unclean, then for him it is unclean. If your brother is distressed because of what you eat, you are no longer acting in love. Do not by your eating destroy your brother for whom Christ died. (Rom. 14:1–4, 13–15)

Sin is violating the Word of God. If for the purposes of your own discipline you wish to have additional standards above and beyond or different from that (but not contrary to it), do not call it sin when you do not keep them, and do not call it sin when someone else does not keep them. The Bible condemns enough sins without us adding to them. These other things will not get forgiven. They *cannot* be forgiven, because they are not sin.

Suppose you have an appointment to meet someone at a certain time, and you are held up by an event beyond your control: a freight train went off the rail and blocked the road, or you had an opportunity to talk to someone and you could not get out of it. You wind up being twenty minutes late. In a case like this, you are not guilty in God's eyes. You were in the will of God waiting for the freight train, or you were in the will of God talking to that person. There is no sin, and therefore there should be no guilt. But you arrived twenty minutes late, and the person who was waiting for you looks at you in an accusing fashion, and you feel guilty. In fact, you probably felt guilty even before you got there, so you already started figuring out an explanation. Even after you explain, you still feel guilty because people generally do not forgive, even though they may acknowledge your explanation. However, your delay was not wrong in the first place.

Imagine now that you did two things in the course of a week. First, you told a big, fat lie. Second, you missed the morning session at a Christian conference by being somewhere else you needed to be. You show up at the conference the next day, and the saints say, "Where were you yesterday?" Let's assume for the sake of argument that you were in the will of God by not being at that conference. You were somewhere God wanted you. When everyone looks at you and says, "Where were you?" you feel guilty. Here you have two guilts:

one, a real sin against a real, holy God, and the other not sin at all. You feel the same guilt for lying as for missing the conference, so you confess both.

God does not have a high view of liars. He tells us that He has prepared a lake of fire for them. But when you confess this lie to the Lord God, He forgives it, and it's gone.

Then you confess missing the conference session, and you still feel guilty. Why? First off, God does not forgive things that are *not sin*. Second, what made you feel guilty was people, and people very often don't forgive. They hold it over you so that you won't do it again. One of the ways you can learn to recognize false guilt is the *lack of forgiveness when you confess it*, when at the same time you have been truly forgiven for other things you did that were morally wrong.

There is another kind of false guilt. That is that when you confessed a real sin to God, God forgave it, and you don't believe it. If you are in this situation, you may not realize that what you are left with is false guilt; you may think it's something else. "It's real guilt, but I wasn't sorry enough," or, "There is some restitution that needs to be done." OK, so check those things out. If it is real guilt, confess it. If there is restitution to be made, take care of it.

If those are not the issues, assume that it's false guilt, no matter how bad you feel about it. Then look in the Scriptures to see if there is anything against this particular thing. In most cases, you won't find it. "There's something against lying." Yes, but you already confessed the lie, and God promised He would forgive you.

When you come to the conclusion (mentally, not spiritually, because you still feel guilty) that you have taken care of it every possible way that you ought to have if it were real guilt, and the guilty feeling is still there, assume that it is from the enemy, and it is false guilt.

How do you get rid of false guilt, then? Confess to God that you feel guilty for being in His will. Confess to *feeling guilty*, because that guilt has taken away your joy, and, in that sense, the false guilt itself is sin. Feeling guilty about false guilt is believing the devil. Believing the devil is sin. Confess *that*. Call *feeling guilty* a sin. "God, I've been believing the devil. He told me this is wrong. He told me You won't forgive it. Please forgive me for believing the enemy."

People who tend toward depression are very likely to be afflicted with false guilt because they pay too much attention to the opinions of men. This guilt that they cannot get rid of leads them into further depression. From there, they can get into false guilt that is very bad, even to the point of thinking their sin is unforgiveable. These Christians are in absolute despair because of what they think they are guilty of. However, they are dead wrong. They are believing the lie of the devil; they feel guilty about forgivable sin that they think is unforgivable.

So they live in *real* guilt, but not the kind of guilt they think. Usually they have a stack of real sins that have been confessed and forgiven by the Lord, but they will not accept the forgiveness. Have you ever heard anyone say, "I can't forgive myself"? That is not the problem. "Can't" means it is impossible. When someone says, "I can't," whatever the sin is, I graciously say, "No, let's say you *won't*. You won't forgive yourself." That is where the real guilt comes in.

Saying you cannot forgive yourself is a euphemism for saying that you are not responsible. You have decided not to forgive yourself because you have a higher standard of sin than God does, and you think your standard is more just. God says you are forgiven, but you say, "Sorry, God, Your standards are not high enough." Make yourself say you *will not*. This thinking is sin in itself and must be repented of.

There are also people who only believe in forgiving themselves after a period of penance—not penance in the Roman Catholic sense, but just feeling miserable about their sin. They do not think it is legitimate to confess and be joyful again right away.

If you are having trouble forgiving yourself, ask yourself if you would forgive someone else who had done the same sin to you. (You might want to say no, but you know that the right answer is yes.) Well then, what is the difference between you and the other person? If you would forgive the one, why will you not forgive the other?

People in this situation refuse to forgive themselves because they are consumed with how awful their sin was. They need to understand that *refusing to forgive is sin*. It is a greater sin than the one they committed originally, because the Scripture says that if you will not forgive, you will not be forgiven. You need to forgive yourself. This does *not* mean saying what you did was right. Forgiveness does not say it was right. Forgiveness says it was wrong, but you are forgiven. *You do not have to think that what you did was OK.* You still have the same view of how wrong it was.

Look at Psalm 51:

> Have mercy on me, O God,
>   according to your unfailing love;
> according to your great compassion
>   blot out my transgressions.
> Wash away all my iniquity
>   and cleanse me from my sin.
> For I know my transgressions,
>   and my sin is always before me.
> Against you, you only, have I sinned
>   and done what is evil in your sight,
> so that you are proved right when you speak
>   and justified when you judge. (vv.1–4)

There are two ways to avoid confessing sin. One is by reducing the enormity of the transgression. A man wants to be forgiven, but he would prefer to be forgiven for something that is not so bad. The other way to avoid confessing is to say that the sin is so bad that he or God or other people cannot forgive it. We either try to make the sin small enough that it is very easily forgivable or so big that it cannot be forgiven.

If the sin is great, it is tempting to think that there is not enough grace for it. But David had a great view of sin and a great view of forgiveness: "Against you, you only, have I sinned and done what is evil in your sight, so that you are proved right when you speak and justified when you judge." Whatever you do to me, God, I deserve it.

But David also says, "Have mercy on me, O God, according to your unfailing love; according to your great compassion blot out my transgressions." David had a very big view of sin and a very big view of God's abundant mercy. He knew that God's mercy was more than enough to cover his sin.

If you have sin that you think is too big, do not minimize the sin. Instead, realize that in relationship to the amount of grace God has made available for us, all it is is sin. Suppose you have committed murder. How are you ever going to get forgiven for that? Simple. It is sin, and God forgives sin. God is a great God, and His grace is *great* grace. Where sin abounds, grace abounds much more. However great your problem is, God is much, much, greater. When a person says, "God forgives me, but I can't forgive myself," he is really saying that he thinks God did not forgive him. He does not want to say that, because it is accusing God of not keeping His promise, but that is what he believes. If he really believed that God forgave him, it would not be that difficult for him to accept the forgiveness.

Sometimes you just have to call the devil a liar.

CHAPTER 6

How to Be Free from Low Self-Esteem

*L*ow self-esteem is a commonly diagnosed problem today. People are told that they do not love themselves enough or that they have an inferiority complex. What I have to say on this issue may sound a little harsh, but it is biblical.

The Scripture says, "Love your neighbor as yourself" (Matt. 22:39). When Jesus quoted this from the Old Testament, He was not commanding us to love ourselves. Self-love is assumed. Jesus' command was to love your neighbor. "I can't love my neighbor until I love myself," you say. That is true—but the man who thinks he does not love himself is deceiving himself. Jesus assumed that *all people love themselves.*

The Bible says, "Husbands, love your wives . . . . After all, no one ever hated his own body, but he feeds and cares for it" (Eph. 5:25, 29).

Picture someone with a characteristic inferiority complex. Now answer me this: whom does that person think about most of the time? *Himself.* What he thinks about is where his love is. The person with an inferiority complex loves himself not too little, but *too much.* If he thought about his neighbor as much as he thinks about himself on a day-to-day basis, that neighbor would be loved to death. His "lack" of self-love is really inordinate self-love.

Suppose you are at a picnic and someone says, "Let's play softball." Why does that guy want to play softball? Because he plays it well. He hits a long ball; he is a good man on the bases. He wants the fun of hitting the ball, and he also does not mind everyone else knowing he can hit it. Then someone else says, "Let's not play softball; let's play horseshoes." Why does he not want to play softball? Because he strikes out, and he does not want everyone else to know it.

The first guy seems to have an extroverted personality or a superiority complex because he plays well. We assume that he has a good view of himself and that the second fellow has a poor view of himself. Hold on a moment. Whom are they both thinking about? The one wants everybody to know how far *he* hits the ball, and the other does not want anybody to know that *he* cannot hit the ball. He may have a poor view of himself when it comes to softball, but he has a good view of himself in that he does not want others to know he is bad at the game. Both people are protecting themselves. Both are thinking of themselves.

Suppose someone is always saying, "I can't do this," and, "I can't do that," and, "How awful I am . . . " He is beating himself up, but his love is still for himself. What he needs to do is get *God's* view of himself. I am not saying he does not have a problem; he *does*. It is just not the problem he thinks he has.

The solution to this is to start thinking about other people, even if you have to do it by deliberate determination. Every time you think of yourself, stop and think of so-and-so, with just as nice thoughts as you would like to think of yourself. The way you think of yourself right now might be derogatory. Aim for a *positive* thinking about someone else instead of *negative* thinking about yourself.

Get your focus off yourself and onto someone else. Suppose you find yourself in a place where you are afraid, e.g., you are sitting in the back seat of a car that someone else is driving along a mountain road, and you're thinking, "This maniac doesn't know how to drive." You wish you were out of the car. What do you do? Start interceding for other people. This applies to everything, not just to fear. Instead of praying for yourself, start praying for *other people*. It gets your mind off your own problems.

This works very well, but the only way to do it is by *choosing* to do it. It will not happen naturally. In fact, it may be very hard to do at first. Stick with it. The more you do it, the easier it will get, because your focus will be more and more on other people.

Intercession for others is not limited to praying; it is any kind of action that you give toward someone else. The best thing to do when you are stuck thinking about yourself is to think of someone who is in worse shape than you. Say, "I think I'll go call on Joe. He's really hurting." I know that in order to help Joe, I need to get grace from God. I get grace from God so that I can help Joe, and at the same time I get grace from God for me.

Other people's problems are one of the primary things that have kept me in good spiritual shape. One night when my youngest son was going to bed, he said, "I think I want to be depressed." He wanted to enjoy the misery. Often when I am out of the joy of the Lord, I will feel like staying there. Frequently, what keeps me from getting this way is other people knocking at my door with their own problems. I know I cannot share my misery with them, so I need to get grace from God for them. When I get grace for them, I get it for myself, too.

Remember that the initial problem was not that you do not love yourself, but that you do. And you love yourself too much in a selfish way. You have too much love, and you are not sharing it. Start sharing.

Next, get God's view of you. Read the Scriptures, and you will find out that God's love for you is not love *because.* Suppose you "don't love yourself" because you have a particular habit you can't shake. Remember that word *can't* from the last chapter. It is wrong. You have a habit that you *won't* shake, so you sit around thinking negative thoughts about yourself. God's view of man is very realistic. He says you are bad news. But He also says, "I love you, and I have many good thoughts toward you." God does not say, "You are good; therefore, I have good thoughts toward you." He says, "You are *bad*; therefore, I have *good* thoughts."

"Many, O Lord my God, are thy wonderful works which thou hast done, and thy thoughts which are to us-ward: they cannot be reckoned up in order unto thee: if I would declare and speak of them, they are more than can be numbered" (Psalm 40:5, KJV). If I tried to speak of all the wondrous deeds that God has done for me and all the wondrous thoughts He has toward me, I could not do it. There are too many. God thinks good things toward me. When I begin to think about myself the way He does, that is a healthy view. Then I find it easier to teach and preach.

Romans 12:3 says, "Do not think of yourself more highly than you ought." It does not say, "more lowly than you ought." The reason it does not say that is that thinking too lowly of ourselves is not our problem. God assumes that we love ourselves, but He does not assume it is healthy when it stops at that. That is a selfish love. That is not God's kind of love toward us. Paul says that if you have God's view of His love toward you, and you go and love others in the same way that you have loved yourself and that God loves you, you have fulfilled the law.

> A new command I give you: Love one another. As I have loved you, so you must love one another. By this all men will know that you are my disciples, if you love one another. (John 13:34–35)

> We love because he first loved us. If anyone says, "I love God," yet hates his brother, he is a liar. For anyone who does not love his brother, whom he has seen, cannot love God, whom he has not seen. And he has given us this command: Whoever loves God must also love his brother. (1 John 4:19–21)

Having a good relationship with God takes care of the selfish thinking called "self-esteem."

Many people wrestle with both kinds of selfish thinking (thinking too highly of themselves but also thinking it is right to feel like a nobody). It can feel natural to assume that when you are in bad shape it is the better, humbler position to think of yourself as a nobody.[3]

These two perspectives can exist either at the same time or back and forth. If they alternate, that does not show that you have gone from loving yourself to not

3. Supposed humility is the same kind of view, and we *all* struggle with this one. We think we are better than other people, even in our humility.

loving yourself. It just shows that there are two different expressions of self-love. The way out is to keep your thoughts on God and on others.

> For by the grace given me I say to every one of you: Do not think of yourself more highly than you ought, but rather think of yourself with sober judgment, in accordance with the measure of faith God has given you. Just as each of us has one body with many members, and these members do not all have the same function, so in Christ we who are many form one body, and each member belongs to all the others. We have different gifts, according to the grace given us. If a man's gift is prophesying, let him use it in proportion to his faith. If it is serving, let him serve; if it is teaching, let him teach; if it is encouraging, let him encourage; if it is contributing to the needs of others, let him give generously; if it is leadership, let him govern diligently; if it is showing mercy, let him do it cheerfully. (Rom. 12:3–8)

Accept the gifts that God has given you, and use them. Do not assume that if you are using what God has given you, you are being an extrovert in a wrong kind of way. Using your gifts is normal. For instance, I believed I should be teaching, but there was a time in my life where if I got up in front of anyone, I would take glory for my ability to do it. Sometimes that still happens, but not like it used to. I have accepted that God has given me this gift, and I am to use it. It is right. It is what God gave it to you for.

If you have a talent and you say, "Using this would draw inordinate attention to myself. I will be humble and not use it," that is wrong. You can think of yourself as being spiritual while you are *not* using your gift and wind up listening to someone else who is using his gift and be critical of him. Do not be critical of him and of yourself and think that you are being spiritual by denying your gifts. Whatever He has given you, use it.

CHAPTER 7

How to Be Free from Anxiety

A nxiety is worrying about the future. It is the fear of living without something. Early in my Christian life, I had several periods of deep and sometimes prolonged anxiety. In each case, someone else pointed me to God and His faithfulness and how to trust Him. In every case, my anxiety ended, and God answered my need.

God cares for us. The more we think about God the way God thinks about Himself, the happier our lives will be. As long as we think of Him according to our accusative thoughts which are not true, we will adjust our lives based upon those lies. We think that God has characteristics that He does not have. We think He is unkind, intolerant, impatient, waiting for us to step out of line so He can swat us. That is not true. He is the opposite: He is kind, faithful, and caring.

> Therefore I tell you, do not worry about your life, what
> you will eat or drink; or about your body, what you
> will wear. Is not life more important than food, and
> the body more important than clothes? Look at the
> birds of the air; they do not sow or reap or store away
> in barns, and yet your heavenly Father feeds them.
> Are you not much more valuable than they? Who of
> you by worrying can add a single hour to his life?
>
> And why do you worry about clothes? See how
> the lilies of the field grow. They do not labor or spin.
> Yet I tell you that not even Solomon in all his splen-
> dor was dressed like one of these. If that is how God
> clothes the grass of the field, which is here today and
> tomorrow is thrown into the fire, will he not much
> more clothe you, O you of little faith? So do not wor-
> ry, saying, "What shall we eat?" or "What shall we
> drink?" or "What shall we wear?" For the pagans
> run after all these things, and your heavenly Father
> knows that you need them. But seek first his king-
> dom and his righteousness, and all these things will
> be given to you as well. Therefore do not worry about
> tomorrow, for tomorrow will worry about itself. Each
> day has enough trouble of its own. (Matt. 6:25–34)

God feeds the birds; they are not anxious. To Him
we are more valuable; He will feed us. God dresses the

flowers in beauty. We are more valuable; He will clothe us. The Father *knows* you need these things. He did not make you with fur. He knows you need clothing. Anxiety about these things is normal for the heathen. We do not want to be like the heathen. We are to seek first the kingdom and His righteousness, and all of these things will be provided.

"Who of you by worrying can add a single hour to his life?" (v. 27). Some people think of worry as a virtue. They think that worrying shows who cares. They look at people who do not worry and think that they don't care. Of course, that might be true. Or not worrying may mean that you believe God's statement that you are more valuable than the sparrows.

"And why do you worry about clothes? See how the flowers of the field grow. They do not labor or spin. Yet I tell you that not even Solomon in all his splendor was dressed like one of these" (vv. 28–29). Jesus is not only talking about clothes; He is talking about pretty clothes, rich clothes, beautiful garments. "If that is how God clothes the grass of the field, which is here today and tomorrow is thrown into the fire, will he not much more clothe you—you of little faith?" (v. 30). You are more important than the grass. Not only are you more valuable than they are, you are *much more* valuable. You need to work, but you can work without worrying. You can work because you are supposed to work.

Scripture is either true or false. If I were to give you a quiz on this passage, you might want to say it is true so you could pass the quiz, but you don't *trust* it. As far as people trust, their real answer is that this is false. Get your gut feeling to agree with the true statement.

One way to do this is to disprove the anxiety. When my son Gordon was fifteen, he spent the summer fighting wildfires. On one of their days off, all the firefighters went to visit a waterfall. They took turns running off the cliff and jumping into the deep water at the bottom of the falls. That cliff didn't go straight down; it went out at an angle. Gordon took a run off the cliff and heard someone yelling behind him, "He's going to hit the rocks!" He started waving his arms to try to get himself away from the cliff face—with the result that he hit the water at a very bad angle.

Gordon knew that if he didn't go back up and jump off the cliff, he would be afraid of jumping for the rest of his life. He was certain that he was going to hit the water wrong again the second time, but he did it anyway. He got past his fear by tackling the fear head-on, not avoiding it. He did something that was frightening and was not afraid. (He did not hit the water wrong the second time.)

Do the things that you're afraid of. Why? Anxiety is almost always a lie. Anxiety lies and tells you bad things will happen if you act. Do it anyway, and you will prove that the anxiety was a lie. If you don't do it, you will continue to think that what the anxiety is telling you is true. Get out on a limb with God. If you're afraid of falling, don't let the fear stop you.

I used to be anxious about money. I could respond to this fear by grasping every penny, trying to make sure I have enough. Or I could follow God's leading in how to use the money I have, and trust that He will continue to provide for my needs. This might look irresponsible to some people. It means that I have spent most of my life not living on a fixed salary. I am dependent on what comes in. When funds are short, I can either be anxious or not be anxious. I seek first the kingdom and choose not to be anxious.

The Bible forbids anxiety. "Do not be anxious about anything, but in everything, by prayer and petition, with thanksgiving, present your requests to God. And the peace of God, which transcends all understanding, will guard your hearts and your minds in Christ Jesus" (Phil. 4:6–7). If we are not anxious for anything, God will give us His peace, which is without comprehension, and which will guard our hearts and minds.

I violated this command on January 1, 1954, and again in 1957. In both cases, God answered my prayer and took care of my needs. When He answered, I was bummed that He had not done it sooner. I was anxious right up to the moment of God's provision, and my worried state meant that I did not rejoice when He took so long to answer my prayer.

Here is what a friend of mine has to say on God's provision:

Elijah, the prophet of Israel (1 Kings 17:1–7), has been sent by God to a wilderness brook far from the burning vengeance of wicked King Ahab. Coming upon him in this scene, we can look briefly at two principles operating in his life: 1) his obedience and 2) his provision from the Lord . . . .

"And the word of the LORD came unto him saying, 'Get thee hence . . . .' So he went . . ." (v. 2–3, 5, KJV). Elijah must have been attuned to the Lord's speaking, or the Word of the Lord could not have come to him. And when it did come, he obeyed instantly. The key to the Christian's guidance is having a heart in tune with the Lord, ready, as Samuel the prophet was, to say, "Speak; for thy servant heareth" (1 Sam. 3:10, KJV). When the word of the Lord is clear to us, are we prepared to act upon it in obedience?

It is to the brook in the wilderness that God commands Elijah to go. But God has already been there ahead of him. He has commanded the ravens to bring Elijah food both morning and evening and has planned for the fresh water of the brook to sustain him. Notice how God works at both ends of the situation. Elijah's provision is there *waiting* for him, *as he obeys.* So it is for the Christian who seeks first the kingdom of God and His righteousness, and consequently finds that all the necessities are added to him (Matt. 6:33).

When the brook dries up, it could well appear to Elijah that God has left him. But at the eleventh hour, "the word of the LORD came unto him" (v. 8) again, to move him on to a new place of provision. God often meets the believer at the eleventh hour. He has not promised grace for anticipation, but rather He assures us, "My grace *is* sufficient" (2 Cor. 12:9, italics mine), right now.

Is our life characterized by the same unquestioning obedience as Elijah's? Are we trusting in the same kind of faithfulness on God's part to meet our need in His own time?[4]

The key verse that my wife Bessie and I relied on together was Matthew 6:33. "So do not worry, saying, 'What shall we eat?' or 'What shall we drink?' or 'What shall we wear?' For the pagans run after all these things, and your heavenly Father knows that you need them" (Matt. 6:31–32). There are two good reasons not to worry. First, the pagans do that. (Do you want to be like a pagan?) Second, your heavenly Father knows you need these things. "But seek first his kingdom and his righteousness, and all these things will be given to you as well" (Matt. 6:33).

There came a day when Bessie and I had a great temptation to be anxious, and we were not anxious. We had been out of the Navy and in Christian work for about a year. We lived in a rented home across the street from a Baptist church in Washington, D.C. It was a nice brick home in a nice community. It was so nice that our next-door neighbor was the former dictator of

4. Howard, Jim, "Obedience & Provision," *The Hammer*, Vol. I No. II, Winter 1982, 9, 16.

Peru. I was talking with him on the sidewalk one day and asked him what he did. He said, "I was *presidente* of Peru, but the people called me *dictator*."

I was responsible for the military work of the Officers' Christian Fellowship on the east coast of the United States. OCF paid us a fixed salary—when there was money in the bank. Payment of the salary was dependent upon sufficient funds coming in to OCF. Normally, we ran about two months behind in salary. That day, we ran out of money.

I had been an officer in the military, and I knew that there were colonels and majors all over D.C. who would have been right there with the funds if they had known we were going without, but we had a strong conviction that we shouldn't tell anyone about our needs. I had learned from George Mueller and Hudson Taylor not to make these needs known except to God.

It was Saturday morning, January 4, 1958. We had three preschool children. Bessie and I realized that we had no money and none of the children's basic food. We had some canned goods, but no perishable food— milk, bread, eggs, orange juice—the things that little children like ours liked to eat.

"So do not worry, saying, 'What shall we eat?' or 'What shall we drink?' or 'What shall we wear?' For the pagans run after all these things, and your heavenly Father knows that you need them. But seek first his kingdom and his righteousness, and all these things will be given to you as well" (Matt. 6:31–33).

We read Matthew 6:25–34 out loud to the Lord. We told Him, "To our knowledge, we are seeking first the kingdom. To our knowledge, we haven't been anxious. You said You know we need these things, so we are taking You at Your word." Then we thanked God. We were meeting His conditions. We rested in that.

The morning mail arrived. In it was an envelope from Lancaster, Pennsylvania, with no return address and no letter. It contained three $1 bills and a tract on hell by Bishop Ryle. We had never been to Lancaster and knew no one there. We thanked God again, and I went to Safeway and bought $2.96 worth of milk, bread, and orange juice. That took us through the weekend.

By Tuesday night, we were again out of milk and bread and still out of money. We gathered the children together and told them that we were out of these two ingredients (and they liked milk and bread!). We explained that what we did in a case like this was to ask God for them. We stood in a circle in the living room.

This time Bessie and I were a little bit more anxious and didn't trust our faith. I did not have enough faith for the prayer, so I asked Douglas if he would pray. He was four and a half years old. In the name of the Lord Jesus Christ, he thanked God for milk and bread. We put baby Heather to bed with half a bottle of milk, the last we had.

We got up the next morning and had pancakes made with no milk and no eggs. After breakfast, I went upstairs to my bedroom office to work on my writing.

There was a knock on the door. Bessie and Douglas answered it. It was the milkman. He said, "I have four quarts of milk for you."

Bessie said, "You must have the wrong address. We didn't order any milk."

"No, I have the right address."

Bessie asked who sent the milk.

"Let's say Santa Claus sent it." (It was just after Christmas.)

Bessie replied, "Let's *not* say Santa Claus sent it. Say the Lord God sent it, and He sent it because this little boy thanked Him for it last night in his prayers." She witnessed to the milkman.

"Are you people Adventists?"

Someone had paid the milkman to deliver to us. Four quarts of milk arrived on Wednesday, six quarts on Friday, four on Monday, every week for the next eleven months. It only quit because we moved to Annapolis, and the dairy didn't deliver that far. To this day, we do not know who paid for it. But whoever did it did not know that little boy had thanked God for it the night before.

We gathered the children in the entryway and presented *Exhibit A: Milk*. We put the milk on the floor, stood in a circle around it, and held a little praise meeting. We thanked God for the milk and reminded Him that we had also asked Him for bread.

I went back upstairs to our room. A few minutes later, Bessie came running up the stairs breathless, waving a $5 bill in her hand. She had been dusting the furniture in the living room and found it underneath a lamp on the end table.

We had no idea how it had gotten there. We did some thinking. The night before (Tuesday), a Navy lieutenant dentist named Scott Smith had come to see me for counseling. He was a brand-new Christian and was really discouraged. We encouraged him and built him up in the faith. He felt he should pay me for the help I had given him, but he thought we would not accept it because we were Christians. We were also living in a nice house, and he thought we might be offended because it did not look like we needed money. But he still felt compelled to give something, so he slid five dollars under the lamp. We bought bread and some other basics with $4.50.

Scott was stationed at the Naval Hospital in Bethesda, Maryland. At the end of our discussion on Tuesday, I had said, "Scott, you need fellowship." He agreed. I said, "Start a Bible study in Bethesda."

"Yeah? With whom?" He didn't think anyone else there would be interested.

"I'll tell you. We will pray right now that God will lead you to two people who want to study the Bible."

"Hahaha! You haven't been to the Naval Hospital much, have you?"

"Let's ask God to lead you to those two officers, and I'll come over tomorrow night to help you start the Bible study." I prayed to that effect. He thought it was the dumbest prayer.

Scott went back to Bethesda. Upon arriving at the Bachelor Officer's Quarters where he lived, he went straight to the men's room with the Bible still in his hand.

Another dentist, Lt. Jim Scribner, saw it. Jim said, "What have you got there?"

"A Bible."

"How about a Bible study? I know someone else who wants to study the Bible, too." (Lt. Scribner was not a Christian.)

On Wednesday morning after the milk arrived, Scott called to tell me of the answered prayer and asked me to driver over to Bethesda that night to help him start the study.

Our '54 Ford was at the mechanic's. It was ready to be picked up, but there was a $15 bill due on it. I also had another bill due that day for $9.50 to be sent out in the mail. That meant I needed $24.50.

We had another prayer meeting and told God that we needed $24.50. The mail arrived. There was a letter from my former roommate on the *USS Hancock*. He had become a Christian when we were serving together in Christmas 1955, three years earlier. He wrote from San Diego, "Jim, I don't know why God wants me to send this to you, but here's twenty-five dollars." I had all the money I had asked for and fifty cents to spare.

Bessie said, "While we're praying, that suit is worn through, and you're coming out of it at the seams. Let's ask God for a new suit."

That night, I went to the Naval Hospital for the Bible study. Lt. Scribner became a Christian during the study.

I told the men I had just gotten out of the Navy.

Scribner said, "You're not in Navy? What did you do with your uniform?" (I had also been a lieutenant.)

I said, "It's hanging in the closet."

"I need a uniform. Would you sell me one? You're my height and my build. I'll give you fifty for it."

I sold it to him for fifty dollars and went to J. C. Penney to look for a new suit. I had his fifty dollars and one dollar left over from the other money we'd received that week. I looked around at all the racks and couldn't find anything I liked.

The salesman came up to me. "You look like a thirty-nine extra-long. I'm sorry; I've only got one suit in that size." He brought it out. It was the only one I liked.

I said, "How much is it?"

"Fifty-one dollars."

I gave him my fifty-one dollars and went home with my new suit.

It was an exciting five days. In my memory, we have not been anxious for money since that Saturday in 1958. That is the way God has taken care of us ever since. The reason it sounds remarkable was because it was one of our first experiences. Things like this have become normal for us. The awful part is it's gotten so normal that we forget to praise God for it. Those five days of being free from anxiety were from simply believing God's Word that He knew our needs. God is faithful. Do not be anxious, and seek His kingdom and His righteousness.

Bessie and I had one wealthy friend whose husband was the manager of a large store. He was a capable, competent businessman and had amassed a great deal of wealth very fast. She had a lot of money at her disposal and was a real fashion plate.

One day, Bessie sent me to the grocery store. We had only $3.03. Bessie made a list of the things we needed. I took Heather, who was in preschool, and we headed off to the store. Like a dumb man, I went around grabbing things off the shelf, forgetting I only had $3.03. I was only getting the things from the list, but it never occurred to me that I needed to add things up in my head as I went to make sure I had enough money to cover it all.

I got through the list and went to the cash register. Heather said, "Dad, can I have a penny for bubble gum?" I reached in my pocket and gave her one of the pennies, and she went off to the gumball machine.

It suddenly occurred to me that I might not have enough money for the groceries. I turned around, and right behind me in line was this wealthy friend with a great, big shopping cart loaded up with all kinds of food. It was too late to get out of line; the cashier was already ringing my things up. I thought, "Oh boy. I'm not going to have enough money for this. I'll to have to take some things back, and there are only a few things in my basket to begin with." I said, "Lord, I don't want to have to do this in front of her. Please bail me out somehow."

The cashier finished ringing my items up and said, "That will be $3.02."

I gave him the three dollars and my two pennies. God cares. *God cares.* It's wonderful.

There are several biblical preventions for anxiety. They are joy, thanksgiving, and casting our anxiety on the Lord. "Rejoice in the Lord always, again I say rejoice" (Phil. 4:4). If you are rejoicing, you cannot be anxious.

It is possible to rejoice always because God gave us the fruit of the Spirit called joy. That happened when we received Christ. Joy is not related to your environment or to events. That is happiness, and it is circumstantial. Joy is related to a constant: the Lord and His salvation. Because He is constant, your joy in Him can be constant, too.

We see this joy in several Scriptures. The first passage describes a state that would be a strong temptation to anxiety.

Though the fig tree does not bud
    and there are no grapes on the vines,
though the olive crop fails
    and the fields produce no food,
though there are no sheep in the pen
    and no cattle in the stalls,
yet I will *rejoice* in the LORD,
    I will be *joyful* in God my Savior. (Hab. 3:17–18)

The Lord your God is with you,
    the Mighty Warrior who saves.
He will take great delight in you;
    in his love he will no longer rebuke you,
    but will rejoice over you with singing.
    (Zeph. 3:17)

The seventy-two returned with joy and said, "Lord, even the demons submit to us in your name."

He replied, "I saw Satan fall like lightning from heaven. I have given you authority to trample on snakes and scorpions and to overcome all the power of the enemy; nothing will harm you. However, do not rejoice that the spirits submit to you, but rejoice that your names are written in heaven." (Luke 10:17–20)

In the same way, I tell you, there is rejoicing in the presence of the angels of God over one sinner who repents. (Luke 15:10)

Restore to me the joy of your salvation
    and grant me a willing spirit, to sustain me.
Then I will teach transgressors your ways,
    so that sinners will turn back to you.
    (Ps. 51:12–13)

What if you cannot rejoice? There is only one biblical reason for losing your joy. It is the chastening of the Lord. "No discipline seems pleasant at the time, but painful. Later on, however, it produces a harvest of righteousness and peace for those who have been trained by it" (Heb. 12:11). When you respond to discipline from God, it yields the peaceful fruit of righteousness, which is joy in the Lord.

Thanksgiving is another means of being free from anxiety. "Give thanks *in all circumstances*; for this is God's will for you in Christ Jesus" (1 Thess. 5:18). This verse tells us to thank God *in* every circumstance (not *for* every circumstance). It is hard to be anxious while you are giving thanks.

"Do not be anxious about anything, but in every situation, by prayer and petition, *with thanksgiving*, present your requests to God. And the peace of God, which transcends all understanding, will guard your hearts and your minds in Christ Jesus" (Phil. 4:6–7). Thank God when you make the request.

I memorized the Philippians passage in 1951. From 1953–54, I was in graduate school in Monterey, California. At Christmastime, I helped set up an Officers' Christian Union conference for officers and their wives at Mt. Hermon over the New Years' weekend. There was an InterVarsity staff conference happening nearby the same weekend, so I asked the director if we could borrow their speaker. We did, and the conference was a blessing.

We held the last meeting on Sunday morning, January 1, 1954. The speaker was a theology student from Germany. His text was Philippians 4:6–7. Because of his accent and the fact that he was teaching on a passage I had memorized, I decided not to pay attention. What could I learn from him?

He read the text and then asked the congregation these questions.

1. How many of you present your requests to God?
2. How many have their petitions answered?
3. How many of you thank God when He answers your prayers?

All of these were answered with a complete show of hands. Then he asked this: "How many of you do not thank God until He answers?"

We were all embarrassed. None of us wanted to raise our hands.

The speaker pointed to the text, where it says that prayers and petitions are to be made *with thanksgiving*. We are to thank God when we make the request. Don't wait until the prayer is answered.

It had been raining hard all weekend. After the last meeting, everyone packed up and went home. I had to stay to settle up the finances. When I was finished, I walked up the mountain to our cabin where Bessie and Douglas (six months old) were waiting. On the way, I saw Roy Grayson with his head under the hood of his 1948 Studebaker. There was a puddle of water around each of his six spark plugs. He was trying to dry them out without much success.

The car was parked under the trees. We decided that we should push it backward out of the trees onto the mountain road. Then Roy would jump into the car and let it run downhill out of gear. As I watched him roll out of sight down the mountain with his engine still not running, I was thankful that he was a pilot!

When his car was out of sight, I went over to my car, a '48 Nash. The starter was underneath the clutch. I stepped on it. The engine turned over once but would not start. I prayed and stepped on the starter again. Nothing. I prayed and tried again. Still nothing. I kept trying. Every time I stepped on the starter, I prayed.

Soon the battery was dead, and no sound came from the engine when I tried the starter. We had to get back to Monterey, and everyone else had already gone. I prayed, "God, what are trying to teach me?"

"What did you learn this morning? 'Make your requests with thanksgiving.'"

I asked God to start the car and thanked Him for it. I tried the starter again. Nothing happened.

I confessed. "God, I was just plugging the formula." This time, I requested and really thanked God. I stepped on the starter, and the engine roared into life.

Bessie and Douglas got in the car, and we drove down the mountain. At the bottom, I saw Roy's car parked on the side of the road. Roy was walking toward us. I said, "Roy, I will give you a push."

"Not necessary," Roy said. "My car is running."

"Guess how I got mine started?" I asked.

"I know. You thanked God. It took me thirty minutes to think of it, too."

I had several other opportunities to believe Philippians 4. But I had to believe something else first; that was 1 Thessalonians 5:18. When I *gave thanks* in all circumstances, I could *rejoice* in the Lord always (Phil. 4:4: "Rejoice in the Lord always. Again I say—rejoice!"). When I was rejoicing and thanking God, then I was able to *be anxious for nothing* (Phil. 4:6).

This was a series of verses I would believe. Each verse caused me to believe the ones connected to it. The basic verse is 1 Thessalonians 5:18, and the key word is *everything*. "In everything give thanks; for this is the will of God in Christ Jesus for you" (NKJV).

Don't worry. Trust God. He knows you need these things. Whether you pray and trust or just trust, in both cases, it is not worrying, and it is trusting Him. But don't ask and worry.

I have done my share of praying and worrying. One time, before the milk and bread event happened, I had to see the chaplain at the Naval Academy. He had been setting up regulations that were preventing Christian work at the Academy. I was trying to get some Christian programs started there, and I had a collision with him. I drove over from D.C. in a snowstorm and spent an hour with him.

When our meeting was over, I returned to the car to find that I had left the lights on, and the battery was dead. I needed a jump or a tow. I only had a nickel with me. It took a dime to use the phone booth. I thought,

"I'll walk over to the math department and see my friend Findley." But Findley wasn't there; he was sick at home. I used the math department phone to call him. He said, "Stay there. I'll send someone to the office to give you ten dollars."

I called a tow truck from the office, and it came and gave me a jump. I drove out to see Findley.

All this time, I was worried and anxious because there was no money at home. I didn't pray. I just went to Findley for money.

When I got home, Bessie said, "You won't believe this, but Joe Carroll is in town, and he wants to see us. I've invited him for dinner, and there isn't anything to give him."

I said, "Don't worry; I've got some money." I went out and bought four quarts of milk, a pound of cheese, two dozen eggs, and the ingredients we needed for dinner. (Again, this was before the other event when we trusted God for milk.)

Joe Carroll arrived. He had bags full of groceries with him: four quarts of milk, a pound of cheese, two dozen eggs. He had bought *exactly* the same things I had. Not only did he have the same things—he even had the same brands. There was no room in the fridge, because I had just filled it up, so we put his things in the snow on the back porch.

I was down in the dumps. I told Joe what had happened that day. He said, "Jim, your problem is that you don't know Philippians 4:6–7. 'Be anxious for nothing, but in everything by prayer and supplication, with thanksgiving, let your requests be made known to God; and the peace of God, which surpasses all understanding, will guard your hearts and minds through Christ Jesus.'"

Of course, I did know it. I'd memorized it years before.

He said, "You don't have the peace of God. How many times has this happened?"

"Lots of times."

"Does He always answer prayer?"

"Yes, but He answers it in such a last-minute way that I can't even rejoice. He always bails me out, but He waits until the final moment to do it."

Joe said, "Your problem is that you didn't start memorizing early enough. You should have started in verse 4: 'Rejoice in the Lord always. Again I will say, rejoice!' What you've been doing is worrying first, praying second, and maybe or maybe not rejoicing when God answers your prayer. That's the reverse order. The Bible says rejoice first, be anxious for nothing second, and pray third with thanksgiving. You've got it backward."

I knew he was right. I said, "OK. How do you rejoice first?"

"Read the Scriptures that have to do with joy, like Philippians and 2 Corinthians."

I felt so guilty about borrowing money from Findley instead of trusting God, especially since Joe's gift had duplicated everything I had borrowed. I had to go to West Point the next day, and I was determined not to use any more of the borrowed money. I had fifty cents of my own, and I used that to get to the train station. I had a rail card from the Officers' Christian Union that covered the train fare.

I took the train to Newark where I was to speak at a CMBC luncheon on my way to West Point. On the train, I read 2 Corinthians. By the time we pulled into Newark, I was exploding with joy.

I said, "God, I hope that hotel I'm speaking at is not on the other side of Newark; I have no idea how I would get there." I walked out of the station, and there it was across the street. I went to the hotel and spoke with great power and joy.

Nine or ten years earlier, when I was a midshipman, I had asked Jack Wyrtzen if he knew any missionaries I could pray for. He said, "Sure. Pray for Dick Hightower. He's a missionary in east Africa, in Kenya." For the rest of my first-class year and on and off for the next decade, I prayed for Dick Hightower. I didn't know who he was, didn't get any of his prayer letters or anything, so I didn't know what to pray, but I prayed for him.

Back to Newark: The luncheon was paid for because I was the speaker, but there was no honorarium. Afterward, I was shaking people's hands, still rejoicing in the Lord. I shook one fellow's hand, and he left twenty dollars in my palm. He was Dick Hightower.

Years later, I told Joe Bayly about this experience. He told me that Dick Hightower was home at that time because several of his children had polio. He was destitute. But he was the one whom God touched to give me the twenty dollars.

With that money, I stayed overnight in the hotel, took the bus to West Point, and returned home.

When you are in a situation like that where there is nothing to do but trust God, you can either worry, or you can trust. My trust *never* came from experience. It always came from the Scriptures. My joy came from 2 Corinthians. My trust came from Matthew 6. "Faith comes by hearing, and hearing by the Word of God" (Rom. 10:17 NKJV). If you don't have faith, get it from the Scriptures. The more you get to know about the character of God, the more you trust Him. The more you know He cares for you, the less you have to worry about yourself. Cast all your cares on Him, for He cares for you. The word "care" means anxiety. Cast all your anxiety on Him, for He is anxious for you. If anyone is going to worry, let God do it. We don't have to worry.

If we know His character and believe what He says in Matthew 6, worry becomes less and less a reality. When you find yourself in situations like I've described, you can be without worry because you know God is going to take care of it—you just don't know how.

I went through many years of having God answer my prayers without being able to rejoice at the answers because I had worried all the time up until He answered it. I still get in these situations now. The difference is now I thank God and say, "Oh boy! I wonder how this one's going to happen." It is from the Word of God that I can do this.

When I tell these stories, people say, "Well, that's Jim Wilson." No. This is from the Scripture. There is nothing unique about me. I have done my share of worrying—too much of it. When I do, I call it sin. I call it not believing God. Worry is calling God a liar.

What do we do when we are already anxious? Anxiety is sin. It is disobedience to clear and rational[5] commands. First, confess the anxiety as sin. Then cast all your anxiety on the Lord. This is the second way to prevent anxiety. "Cast all your anxiety on him because he cares for you" (1 Pet. 5:7). God cares for you.

When we are anxious, we become immobilized. We cannot make decisions. If we do make a decision, we have no confidence that it is the right one. If the decision is doubtful, it is sin.

Anxiety is the opposite of faith and the opposite of hope. Hope is a glad anticipation of something wonderful in the future, something that is sure to happen. "While we wait for the blessed hope—the appearing of the glory of our great God and Savior, Jesus Christ" (Titus 2:13). Anxiety is also an emotion about the future—about something that is negative and unpleasant and may not even happen.

Hope is a promise of God. Anxiety is a lie of Satan. Anxiety is not a problem. Anxiety is not just a bad habit; it is *sin.*

---

5. God gives us reasons for the commands related to anxiety; but even if He hadn't, we would still need to obey them, because they are commands.

If we confess our sins, he is faithful and just and will
forgive us our sins and purify us from all unrighteousness. (1 John 1:9)

My dear children, I write this to you so that you will
not sin. But if anybody does sin, we have an advo-
cate with the Father—Jesus Christ, the Righteous
One. (1 John 2:1)

God is faithful to forgive sins if we confess them.
Don't ask God for forgiveness. When we do that, we are
telling God that we think He has the option to not forgive sin. He does not have that option. He *promised* to
forgive us, and He paid for the sins first. He is faithful.
Confess and rest in His forgiveness.

The solution for anxiety is to rejoice in the Lord always (Phil. 4:4). It is not possible to be anxious when
we are rejoicing in Him.

CHAPTER 8

How to Be Free from Anger and Fits of Rage

"In your anger do not sin": Do not let the sun go down while you are still angry, and do not give the devil a foothold . . . . *Get rid of all bitterness, rage and anger*, brawling and slander, along with every form of malice. Be kind and compassionate to one another, forgiving each other, just as in Christ God forgave you. (Eph. 4:26–27, 31–32)

Anger is both an internal state and an event. It can be divided into several gradations: anger inside; expressing that anger, either toward people or toward the wall or the floor; and a fit of rage—losing your temper. Losing your temper is always an event, and it is produced by anger. A person who has no anger inside will never lose their temper.

The Scriptures tell us to get rid of both the internal anger and the events it causes. "But now you must rid yourselves of all such things as these: anger, rage, malice, slander, and filthy language from your lips." (Col. 3:8).

"The acts of the sinful nature are obvious: sexual immorality, impurity and debauchery; idolatry and witchcraft; hatred, discord, jealousy, fits of rage, selfish ambition, dissensions, factions and envy; drunkenness, orgies, and the like. I warn you, as I did before, that *those who live like this will not inherit the kingdom of God*" (Gal. 5:19–21). When I counsel people, I often ask them to read this passage. Then I ask how many of these words describe them. The text says that people who live like this will not inherit the kingdom of God. This way of life is normal for non-Christians. Here is the problem. Christians also have fits of rage, and they are not allowed to.

Many Christian husbands verbally abuse their wives. Oftentimes, the wives just give it right back to them. The other families in church don't know what is going on until suddenly there is a divorce. It goes that far because people do not get rid of the anger in their hearts.

When it comes to anger, there are two kinds of people: those who get angry, lose their temper, and forget about it, and those who get angry and hate you for life. The person who gets angry and loses his temper causes everyone else to hate him for life, and he doesn't understand why, because he's over it. That is one reason it is wrong to express anger. It can make other people angry for a long time. Fits of rage cause great harm to wives and children.

Although men tend to have the most trouble in the area, women are also subject to fits of rage. They keep a store of anger inside so it is ready to use as a defense mechanism, or it is kept in reserve to be a threat to anyone who wants peace in the family.

I have personally witnessed several very scary fits of rage. One time I went to confront a pastor who was having an affair. He had gone to his wife's mobile home to visit his teenage daughters. I heard that he was going, so I made certain that I was present. He did not respond to me in anger, but he went into a fit of rage with his wife and his adopted daughter. She said to him, "Daddy, I love you."

He replied with anger, "You don't love me!"

When he left, he was still so dangerous that I locked the door behind him. He came back and pounded on the door very hard, then began to rock the trailer. He married the other woman. Ten years later, he repented.

Many years ago, Bessie and I went together to see a married couple we were hoping to reconcile. The "other woman" was there, and she went berserk. No one was hurt; she took it out on the car. She was not a Christian.

Another time, a man came into our bookstore to inform me that he was going to kill his wife. We managed to hide her until his fit of rage was over. He was not a Christian.

A fit of rage is a mark of the unregenerate man (Gal. 5:20). In young children, it is called a tantrum. You can call it "losing it" or "going ballistic" or being "short-fused." These are euphemisms. Many people have short fuses. Some take pride in being quick to anger. Their friends and relatives learn to walk softly or give them a wide berth. They hold their families hostage to a wrath which can erupt any time.

In recent months, I have encountered several men who live with anger smoldering inside. Here are a few things I've been told by or about them. (All of these statements are about *Christian* men.) "He has only one emotion, and that's anger"; "I've been angry all my life"; "I lose my temper with my wife once a week"; "I am improved. I only beat my wife once a week"; "By court order, I am not allowed to marry the mother of my children because of my anger."

Which of these lists describes you best?

> The acts of the sinful nature are obvious: sexual immorality, impurity and debauchery; idolatry and witchcraft; hatred, discord, jealousy, *fits of rage*, selfish ambition, dissensions, factions and envy; drunkenness, orgies, and the like. I warn you, as I did before, that those who live like this will not inherit the kingdom of God. (Gal. 5:19–21)

> But the fruit of the Spirit is love, joy, peace, patience, kindness, goodness, faithfulness, gentleness and *self-control*. Against such things there is no law.

Those who belong to Christ Jesus have crucified the sinful nature with its passions and desires. Since we live by the Spirit, let us keep in step with the Spirit. (Gal. 5:22–25)

The opposite of the acts of the sinful nature is the fruit of the Spirit. Self-control is obviously the opposite of a fit of rage. However, it is not the only opposite. Someone who has lost their temper is not loving, joyful, peaceful, patient, kind, good, faithful, or gentle. Rage undoes *all* the fruit of the Spirit. That is why such fits are natural for people who are not born of the Spirit. The obvious explanation for someone with this kind of anger problem is that he is not saved.

When a person is saved, he is transferred from verses 19–21 to verse 22. The things in the first list are replaced with the fruit of the Spirit. You cannot have them both. I cannot have self-control and a fit of rage at the same time. I cannot have bitterness and love, joy, and peace at the same time. You might think you are in both lists, but you aren't really. If I am impatient, am I kind and loving? No. If you, as a Christian, find yourself back in the first list, confess it.

Being a Christian is the essential condition for preventing fits of rage. Unbelievers can express anger, but they cannot get rid of it without repentance. The unbeliever needs to repent of his sins to God, confess that Jesus Christ is Lord, and believe in his heart that Christ died for his sins and rose from the dead.

He told them, "This is what is written: The Christ will suffer and rise from the dead on the third day, and repentance and forgiveness of sins will be preached in his name to all nations, beginning at Jerusalem." (Luke 24:46–47)

If you confess with your mouth, "Jesus is Lord," and believe in your heart that God raised him from the dead, you will be saved. (Rom. 10:9)

"Let all bitterness, wrath, anger, clamor, and evil speaking be put away from you, with all malice. And be kind to one another, *tenderhearted*, forgiving one another, even as God in Christ forgave you" (Eph. 4:31–32 NKJV). You cannot have anger and wrath inside you and be tenderhearted at the same time. You have to get rid of the first in order to do the second.

"But now you yourselves are to *put off all these: anger, wrath*, malice, blasphemy, filthy language out of your mouth" (Col. 3:8 NKJV). This command is based on what the first part of the chapter talks about: "Since, then, you have been raised with Christ, *set your hearts on things above*, where Christ is seated at the right hand of God. Set your minds on things above, not on earthly things. For you died, and your life is now hidden with Christ in God" (Col. 3:1–3). If you are a Christian, you have died, and your life is hidden with Christ in God. *Therefore*, do not do these things; they belong to the nonbeliever. You are born again of the Holy Spirit; don't be angry. However, to be rid of your anger, you have to call it sin, confess it, and forsake it.

It is a common Christian doctrine that when a person receives Christ, he receives a new nature but also retains the old nature. That is not true. The truth is that the old man is dead. "Do not lie to one another, since *you have put off the old man with his deeds*" (Col. 3:8). Do not lie, because you *don't* have the old self. ". . . and have put on the new man who is renewed in knowledge according to the image of Him who created him" (Col. 3:9). The idea that you still have the old self is not biblical. The old man has been crucified. He is dead.

Christian culture tells us that we sin because of the remaining old nature. That is not true. We sin without the old nature, and we do it in direct disobedience to God. "Because of these things the wrath of God is coming upon the sons of disobedience" (Col. 3:6). You should not have the characteristics of a nonbeliever. God does not tolerate them in Christians, because we have died to sin in Christ. Blaming things on the old nature is just an excuse for sin—but it's an excuse we don't have.

"O foolish Galatians! Who has bewitched you that you should not obey the truth, before whose eyes Jesus Christ was clearly portrayed among you as crucified? This only I want to learn from you: Did you receive the Spirit by the works of the law, or by the hearing of faith? Are you so foolish? Having begun in the Spirit, are you now being made perfect by the flesh? Have you suffered so many things in vain—if indeed it was in vain?" (Gal. 3:1–5 NKJV). You dumbbells! You not-so-smart Galatians! How did you get into the kingdom? You were washed clean from your sins by grace: why do you think keeping clean is done by hard work? You got in by grace through faith, and you walk by grace through faith. The Galatians got in for free, and they were trying to work it off.

"If anyone slaps you on the right cheek, turn to him the other also" (Matt. 5:39, ESV). If I've got this command rolling around in my head, and a man comes up and smacks me in the face, I can say to myself, "I know what the verse says," and smack him back. Knowing right from wrong does not make me do what is right. However, if I take that verse of Scripture and put it in my heart, when he smites me on the right cheek, I turn the other cheek. Make the commands *part* of you. How? Put that command in your head and *thank God for it* all day long. That will get it into your heart. When we have the fruit of the Spirit in our hearts, and we are tempted, it is generally easy to resist. There will be love, joy, and peace in your heart, and it will be a no-brainer to obey. You won't have to think about it; you will just respond rightly.

Suppose someone lies about you and spreads it all over town. Matthew 5:11 says to rejoice and be exceedingly glad when you are slandered. Think, "That poor guy. He's in spiritual big trouble. I wonder what I can do to help him." Don't let his sin tempt you to sin. Start praying for him. Don't let his lie affect you. If it does, it is because you love yourself too much.

"If anyone forces you to go one mile, go with him two miles" (Matt. 5:41, ESV). Double the cheeks, double the miles, double the shirts. Suppose a man says, "I hate you. I'm going to sue you." Do you say, "Sue away! I'll countersue." If you do that, what are your chances of leading that person to Jesus? Not good. He may not come to Christ anyway, but if you act like that, I can almost guarantee you he won't. Fighting back helps him justify himself in his own mind. Giving in makes him feel guilty.

Most euphemisms are meant to lessen the sense of guilt. However, there is one euphemism for anger that is made to increase it. It is the term "pissed" or "pissed off." Using this term is doubly wrong because it justifies anger ("I am guilty of anger *and rightly so.*"), and it is unclean language. It is vulgar in all uses, and yet I have heard Christians use it. "And walk in the way of love, just as Christ loved us and gave himself up for us as a fragrant offering and sacrifice to God. But among you there must not be even a hint of sexual immorality, *or of any kind of impurity,* or of greed, because these are improper for God's holy people" (Eph. 5:2–3 NKJV).

There is *nothing* that can justify losing your temper. If you are born of the Spirit, a fit of rage is neither normal nor acceptable. So why do Christians lose their tempers? If they are truly Christians, they have accumulated numerous little sins which they have not confessed and consequently not received forgiveness for. This leaves them ready to give in to a slight temptation with a whopping fit of rage.

David describes the buildup this way: "Keep your servant also from willful sins; may they not rule over me. Then will I be blameless, innocent of great transgression" (Psalm 19:13). Notice that the description is one of *prevention.* The Christian who is prone to fits of rage has not been eager to be kept from willful sins. He has allowed them to rule over him.

You can prevent fits of rage, but not without complete confession and repentance of all your previous fits of rage. This confession must be made without any euphemisms to minimize your sin, and it must also include the willful sins that led up to your anger.

How do you get rid of the built-up anger? Anger management classes don't solve the problem. First, they tell you that anger is good. Second, they tell you that you have to let it out in a non-hurtful way. I read an article in a major newspaper which said, "Healthy anger causes all kinds of dysfunctional actions." The author listed them: yelling, screaming, putting people down, throwing things. He said that *healthy* anger produces these unhealthy acts. He said that the solution is to teach people that the anger is not the problem; the problem is not knowing how to release it.

How do you release it? It is a common but mistaken belief that you can get rid of anger by expressing it. Counselors tend to fall into this trap.

Many years ago, I was asked to speak on a panel of three at Washington State University called The Nosebag Group (a brown bag lunch group). The two other panel members were Ph.D. candidates in psychology and counseling at WSU. The subject was releasing anger.

I said, "Isn't that going to be harmful to the other person?"

"No. We just tell them to pretend that this chair is your father, and this pillow is a club. Then you go beat your father with a club—but you're really beating that chair with a pillow. You're not hurting your father; you are just getting the anger expressed."

Beating the chair does not take the anger away. It is still there. Someday you will run into your father, and you won't have a pillow.

These men claimed that there was a healthy way of expressing anger, as if expressing it was good. The Bible says to *get rid* of anger. You don't get rid of anger by articulating it. That's how murder takes place.

A long time ago, I got to know a young couple and led the wife to Christ. Her husband had been a Christian since he was sixteen but had been out of fellowship for ten years. He got back in fellowship and spent many years in the Navy. When he left the Navy, he went to seminary, graduated, and joined a church. He became the pastor there in the fall and immediately fell in love with the church secretary. He had an affair with her in November, confessed in February, was defrocked in March, and got divorced.

I went to see them both six months later. I asked the wife what she had been doing since the divorce. She said she had been going to group therapy. I asked her what was happening in the therapy sessions.

She said, "I'm getting rid of a lot of anger!"

"Oh," I said, "Is it gone?"

She had spent six months pouring out her anger on other sick people who were pouring out their anger on her. They were just messing each other up.

"Is it gone?"

"No."

"'Getting rid of it' isn't getting rid of it. The Bible says to get rid of anger, and it doesn't mean six months from now. You do not get rid of anger by expressing it. You get rid of it by confessing it as a violation of the holiness of God. It is great sin. It does not matter how much sin the other person is in. Your sin is *your* sin, and it is forgivable only if you confess it. Get rid of your anger now."

She did. She went back to group therapy, and she had nothing to say. The other members and the psychiatrist were convinced that she was suppressing her anger. She wasn't—it was forgiven, and it was gone.

Once you are rid of your anger, focus on prevention. The primary preventative is living in the holiness of God. Walk in the light. Sanctify the Lord in your heart. "But in your hearts set apart Christ as Lord. Always be prepared to give an answer to everyone who asks you to give the reason for the hope that you have. But do this with gentleness and respect" (1 Pet. 3:15). Keep the fruit of the Spirit by 1) keeping sins confessed up to date, 2) filling up your heart with good things from the Word of God, and 3) praying for your enemies. When you are praying for someone, you cannot be filled with malice toward him.

Do not have a light view of sin. Romans 7:13 (NKJV) describes sin as being "exceedingly sinful." Recognize anger as a violation of God's holiness. It is sin of the worst kind. The devil takes over, and you have no control once it starts.

What if anger has been a habit your whole life? Maybe you have always had a temper. You might even brag about it. ("I've got a temper," "I'm a redhead," or "I'm Irish.") We assume that losing our temper is like being short or tall. It's the way we were born, the way we are.

I have one grandchild who was born complaining. I saw that child turned around before he was three years old. In first grade, he got high marks for being the most Christian-acting kid in his class. Some people are born with a shorter fuse than others, but that is not an adequate justification for getting angry. Anger is not normal. No matter how you were born, once you receive the Lord Jesus Christ, you are indwelt with the Holy Spirit, and you must get rid of anger. Break the habit by calling it what it is. Call it sin.

I used to have fits of rage before I was converted, and I have lost my temper three times since I was converted. (I have been angry more than that, but only lost my temper three times.) All three were in 1948, the year after my conversion. The first two times, I blasted people with words, and the third time I hit someone. I was with my girlfriend. She saw that I was getting very, very angry, so she started to laugh to try to cool me down. It had the opposite effect. She bent over to reach something. Her rump was sticking up, and I hit it—hard. It was a fit of rage. And I was a Christian. I thought, "No more." It is *not acceptable at all*. It is an evil sin. It has not happened since.

When you start calling it sin after you lose your temper, you will soon be calling it sin *before* you lose your temper. Get grace before you get angry. If you were angry yesterday, very likely you will be tempted the same way today. Before you get out of bed in the morning, have a pre-quiet time quiet time. It's dangerous out there. When you wake up, ask God for grace before the temptation.

When you confess anger after the fact, your confession must cover more than the outburst. It must cover the cause down inside, and you must forsake that cause. Otherwise your confession is glib and shallow. I am not speaking of remorse or penance. I am speaking of godly sorrow as described in 2 Corinthians 7:10: "Godly sorrow brings repentance that leads to salvation and *leaves no regret*, but worldly sorrow brings death."

Why do you get angry?

- Things don't go my way.
- Someone stepped on my rights.
- A situation is out of my control.
- I am frustrated.
- I am tired or in pain.
- Injustice has been done to someone else.
- I am not being listened to.
- Someone has hurt my feelings.

The common denominator in nearly all of these is "me." *I* am not being listened to, someone hurt *me*. Injustice toward someone else is the only one of these that could possibly be a Christian reason for anger.

Why do people get into fights? Because they have hurt each other's feelings or stepped on each other's rights. Both are angry, and each one thinks he is right, because he has been hurt. Don't I have any rights? The answer is no. The Christian has no rights such that he can be mad when they are violated. The Constitution allows for rights, but God does not. There are things that *God* will take care of for you, but not that you are to take care of yourself.

"Do not let any unwholesome talk come out of your mouths, but only what is helpful for others, for building others up according to their needs, that it may benefit those who listen" (Eph. 4:29). Do we talk because we want the floor, or because what we have to say is going to build someone else up? When we express anger, it is always for our own benefit. It is never for the other person's good. It tears him down.

"My dear brothers, take note of this: Everyone should be quick to listen, slow to speak and slow to become angry, for man's anger does not bring about the righteous life that God desires" (James 1:19–20). When you express anger, you assume that you are right, and the other person is wrong. When you deal with your anger before God, you assume that you are wrong, and you come to Him for forgiveness. Coming to Him is turning away from anger, and He takes it away.

People are quick to anger because they love themselves too much. "I'm too nice a guy to be treated this way!" They keep a reserve of anger down in their hearts as a defense mechanism.

Society today is concerned about people not loving themselves enough. That has never been a problem. People love themselves too much. Don't have such a high opinion of yourself that you feel the need to be self-protective. The times I've been angry in the last few decades, I was embarrassed. I've been a Christian for decades, and I'm still angry! As I look back at those times, I see that it was for no other reason than thinking of myself.

Low self-esteem, low self-love, and low self-worth are terms that were invented in the late twentieth century; they were never heard of before that. Picture someone who has low self-esteem. About whom is that person thinking most of the time? Himself. His problem is not low self-esteem. His problem is high self-esteem. He loves himself, not too little, but too much.

Psychologists say that in order to love someone else, you need to love yourself first. Scripture tells us to love our neighbors as we love ourselves. According to Jesus, loving yourself is a given. Ephesians 5 says no one ever hated his own flesh. If a person with low self-esteem loved his neighbor as much as he loves himself, the neighbor would be loved to death. But he can't do that—not because he doesn't have much love for himself, but because he has so much that he is busy thinking about himself all the time.

However, you do not have to have inordinate self-esteem to get angry. All you need is *normal* self-esteem, which is too much. The Bible teaches us, "Do not think of yourself more highly than you ought" (Rom. 12:3). God is not worried about anyone thinking of himself more lowly than he ought to think.

Look at the situation from the other person's perspective. Suppose you get mistreated (or think you were mistreated), and you get angry. Then think this: "Suppose I did to someone else what that person just did to me. How would I feel? Would I feel glad or sad?" Would you feel more awful if you did it to someone else, or if it was done to you? Most of us recognize that we would feel awful if we did that to someone else. Say, "If I did that, I would be really convicted of sin. This poor person must be really convicted. He needs help. I wonder what I can do to help him."

What if you are angry with God? What you are saying is, "God, I'm too important for You to treat me like this." You are holding Him responsible who is just and merciful and kind. That is sin. Suppose God took offense at what you were doing there. You might be in big trouble. God understands that kind of anger, but He does not justify it, short of you confessing it as sin.

It is possible to not lose your temper when you are upset. A Christian who periodically loses his temper generally does it for two reasons: he has it down in his heart all the time, and it comes to the surface when he gets cross. "A good man brings good things out of the good stored up in his heart, and an evil man brings evil things out of the evil stored up in his heart. For the mouth speaks what the heart is full of" (Luke 6:45).

We always have an excuse for losing our temper, but what is the reality? Evil lies at the door. There is evil in you *before* you lose your temper. If your heart is filled with righteousness and light, that comes out. When anger comes out, it tells you that that is what was in your heart before you got angry. You had it in reserve in case you needed it in the future. The solution is to keep your heart *filled up with good things* all the time. If something catches you by surprise, it should make good things pop out.

In general, people do not want to be filled with good things. They would rather say something strong and unkind. They would rather sin and confess than prevent it from happening in the first place. Being angry is not a Christian option. We are told to be kind to one another.

I was at a three-day prayer conference for pastors in western Washington. We prayed and sang for two and a half hours in the morning, prayed for two and a half hours in the afternoon and two and a half in the evening, and we had communion every night. We prayed for each other and for each other's families. Quite a few denominations were represented there. It was a wonderful time.

Each night, someone was in charge of communion, but we never announced who it was. One of us was just asked each night by the person who was in charge. Evening came, and we were singing. The fellow who had been put in charge for that evening said, "Let's have some quiet." None of us knew he was in charge, so someone else said, "Let's sing such-and-such," and we went on singing and rejoicing and praising God and testifying.

Finally, he just blew up. "I'm in charge of this communion, and I wanted to have a nice, quiet, peaceful time, and here you guys are confessing sins and singing hymns!" Of course, he had to confess he had sinned before he could take communion, which he did.

It made me wonder, in all the time he was steaming about this, why hadn't he confessed it before he blew up? He wanted to let us know that he was angry and confess it afterward. That is often the way we are. "I'm angry. I could confess this anger, but if I do, I won't get to express it, and I want these people to hear it." You let it out and confess it later. In the meantime, you wipe out everyone else. You could have confessed it beforehand and not done that.

Soak yourself in Scripture. Fill up your heart with good things. Work on your attitude. You must care enough to keep from sinning and destroying everyone in sight, including yourself.

The temptation to be angry is stronger when we are tired, in pain, or hungry (or, for women, when it's the wrong time of the month).

I had been married a few months, and I had a problem. Like all young husbands, I was dumb. For the life of me, I couldn't figure out why something could be funny to Bessie twenty-five days of the month and a complete tragedy the other five.

I was dumb, but I could figure, and I finally figured it out. I said, "Bessie, is this event predictable?"

"Yes."

"You mean you know thirty days in advance when you're going to lose it?"

She didn't quite like it being put that way, but she said yes.

"You have that much advance preparation, and it still catches you off guard?"

That seemed normal to her, but it didn't seem normal to me. I said, "What we will do is you let me know in advance when this is going to happen, and I will walk softly. I will be kind and considerate, and I will pray with you for grace during this period."

It worked wonderfully. You cannot change the hormones, but the hormones are just a temptation. It does not mean you have to sin. Men do not have anything that will produce a chemical temptation quite like this, but if you want to understand what the women are going through, here's a way to get close. First, have someone keep you up all night; then don't allow yourself *any* food or caffeine the next day. That will produce a chemical event in your body that will make you act in a similar fashion.

Pain, tiredness, hunger, and hormones are chemical reactions that can make us irritable. All they are is temptation. You do not have to sin because you are tempted.

I knew one woman who was the wife of a medical doctor. She got right with the Lord, and her husband became a Christian. Yet she had a violent temper. I remember going out to her house one time to keep her from killing her gardener. I bailed her out of jail, and she passed out in our bathroom. Another time she called, hysterical. I asked her what the problem was.

She said, "I'm going to shoot my husband."

"Why are you calling me?"

"I thought you might come up with a reason why I shouldn't."

"What's the problem?"

"I found a woman's comb in the car. I know whose it is, and I know when it happened. When he comes home tonight, I'm going to shoot him." She was completely capable of doing that.

I said, "For all I know, he could have been unfaithful many times, especially back before he was a Christian. But I will guarantee you that this time he is absolutely innocent."

"Why is that?"

"I've known the devil for a long time, and the one time he would have you shoot your husband is when he's not guilty. That's the way the devil works."

"What should I do?"

"Put the comb back in the car and forget it."

She put the comb back in the car, but she didn't forget it. She was steaming all day. In the middle of the afternoon, she thought, "If I take a hot bath, that will take it out of me." Of course, the solution was to *confess the sin* and watch it disappear, but she thought she would cook it out of herself instead. She was in the bathroom when her thirteen-year-old daughter came home from school and yelled out, "Mom, have you seen my new comb?"

She said, "Look in the car."

I asked her husband if he knew why his wife was that way. He hadn't the faintest idea. "Do you know when she has her period?" He started thinking and realized that all of her rage happened at that time of the month. He had never put it together before—and he was a doctor! He was so wrapped up in each crisis that he didn't stop to think why they were happening.

If you have a problem like this, consider it a temptation. Temptations are not sin. You can get preventative grace to protect you in them. You do not have to sin first. When I need to be up all night, I know that I am going to be tempted to irritability, so I pray for grace in advance. Even in ordinary circumstances, I do this. Before I get up in the morning, I pray for grace for whatever comes up, because it's dangerous out there. You can rely on God's grace: abundant grace, overflowing grace, preventative grace. It is not there just to pick up the pieces.

Feelings happen, and they can happen quickly, but some of the bad feeling will be prevented by you being "graced up" in advance. If I am too quick to anger, it is generally because something was already wrong *before* I got angry. If I am graced up, when someone does something that would normally hurt my feelings, I can say, "Oh, that poor guy. If I did something like that, I would feel awful. He must feel awful. I wonder what I can do to help him."

"In your anger do not sin . . . " (Eph. 4:26). It is possible for anger to be righteous, but it is only a remote possibility. (Rage is never righteous.) The King James says, "Be angry, and do not sin" (NKJV). I have left this topic for the end of the chapter, because while anger can be righteous, it is very rare. Most of the anger people think is justified is *not*.

What is righteous anger? Suppose I am walking down the street, and someone comes up and hits me very hard and knocks me to the ground. What is my natural reaction? Get up and knock him to the ground! That is a natural response. What does Jesus say to do? Turn the other cheek. Do something that is not natural. Do something that is supernatural. He said to turn the other cheek, and He meant turn it with real love and kindness. That means that if I hit the other guy back, or even *want* to hit him back, I am in sin. God says to return good for evil and to rejoice when you are persecuted. "If someone strikes you on the right cheek, turn to him the other also. And if someone wants to sue you and take your tunic, let him have your cloak as well. If someone forces you to go one mile, go with him two miles. Give to the one who asks you, and do not turn away from the one who wants to borrow from you" (Matt. 5:39–42).

What if the other person is evil? This passage assumes that he is evil. He is not punching you in the face because he's a nice guy! He is doing it for an evil reason. Just before this, Jesus says, "Do not resist an evil person" (Matt. 5:39). This is unusual teaching. We Christians say we believe the Bible from cover to cover—until we have to obey it. Then we discover exception clauses. We come up with special reasons not to obey the hard commands. So I get angry when I get hit. But it is unrighteous anger.

Now suppose I am walking down the street with my wife or my grandmother, and someone comes along and knocks *her* flat. Do I say, "Well, it's none of my business," and walk off? Do I pick her up and turn her around so he can hit her on the other cheek? No. It is not my job to help Grandma be Christian; it is my job to protect her. This would be a right time to be angry. There are righteous ways to respond to an evil person, and that includes being allowed to protect other people with force.

However, we are very seldom angry when someone else is hurt. We tend to get angry only when *we* are
hurt. I can recall being angry on someone else's behalf
only one time in my life. But I have been angry lots of
times. I call those sin. How do I know they are sin? The
Scripture says, "Rejoice in the Lord always" (Phil. 4:4).
Am I rejoicing in the Lord when I am doing this? I cannot recall a single time in my life when I personally was
offended and got angry and was innocent in my anger.
That does not mean the other guy was right in those
situations; it just means I wasn't right. The Bible allows
for the other person being evil; it does not allow us to
be evil back.

"The wrath of man does not produce the righteousness of God" (James 1:20 NKJV). Let's take a look at
someone whose anger actually was righteous—Jesus.
The only mention of Jesus being angry in the Scriptures
is in Mark 3. "He looked around at them in anger and,
deeply distressed at their stubborn hearts, said to the
man, 'Stretch out your hand.' He stretched it out, and
his hand was completely restored" (Mark 3:5).

Jesus was angry because of the hardness of their
hearts. The Sabbath was made for man, not man
for the Sabbath, and the Son of Man is Lord of the
Sabbath. Jesus asked the Pharisees if it was lawful to
do good on the Sabbath or to do harm. They kept silent. The Pharisees watched him to see if He would
do good on the Sabbath. That is when Jesus got angry and healed the man with the withered hand. The

Pharisees immediately went out to conspire with the Herodians to kill Jesus.

Looked at what happened when Jesus got angry. He *healed* someone. When we get angry (even with what we think is righteous anger), what usually happens? We hurt people. We break stuff. When Jesus got angry, he fixed something.

When you get angry, and you think you have a right to be angry, what are the results? Does your anger hurt, or does it restore?

"'In your anger do not sin': Do not let the sun go down while you are still angry" (Eph. 4:26). How do I keep the sun from going down? Do I get a jack and say, "Sun, you can't go down; I'm still angry"? Even if it is good anger, you have to get rid of it before sundown. Righteous anger is like manna—it rots overnight.

Some time ago, I was talking to a Christian father whose daughter had been abused. When he found out about the abuse, he was very angry. I went to see him. "You have until sundown to get rid of the anger."

He said, "I know."

It took him until three a.m., but he got over it. He knew that his anger was no longer within the bounds of not sinning and that he was capable of killing the man who had abused his daughter.

God gave us three outlets for our emotions: laughter, tears, and anger. They are like the escape valve on a pressure cooker. It lets the steam out so the cooker doesn't blow. God designed them that way. Sometimes when I am speaking on a very serious subject, I will say something to make the audience laugh—not because I want to make light of what I am talking about, but because I want to ease the pressure on the people. God allows us to express these things spontaneously, but He does not allow us to sin with the expression.

Suppose you find someone who when you told him a joke, laughed all day, all night, all the next day, and the day after that. You would know that there was something wrong with him. Laughter is spontaneous, and then laughter *ends*. Tears are spontaneous, and then tears end. If someone cries night and day, something is wrong. Anger is the same. Healthy anger is an escape valve. It is slow to happen, it is without sin, and it does not last past sundown. Even when your anger is righteous, you must not keep on being angry.

Many people do not quit being angry. Day and night for years, they are angry. They are filled with anger, and they take it out on whoever is close by. Since God commands, "Do not let the sun go down while you are still angry," there must be a way to stop anger. It doesn't have to go on for months; it does not even have to wait until tomorrow morning.

I remember one time when I went to bed angry. One of my sons had disobeyed me. He came home late in the evening while I was doing marriage counseling, and I saw at once that he had been disobedient all day. I became immediately angry. But I was in the middle of a counseling session! I excused myself for a moment, went into the kitchen, and asked Bessie to pray for me because I was in bad shape.

The couple I was counseling stayed and stayed and stayed. I wanted to get away and go lay it on my teenage son. Bessie prayed for me. I went to bed angry, thinking that I would sleep it off. I woke up angry. I thought, "I'll go run a mile and a half and burn it out." I was angry every step of the way. "Well, I need some time with the Lord. I'll go to work." I was running a textbook store at a Christian college.

Before I left for work, Bessie said, "I think you'd better talk to him."

I said, "I am in no condition to talk to him. The Scripture says, 'If any man be overtaken in a fault, you who are spiritual restore such a one in a spirit of meekness.' I'm not spiritual, and I'm not meek. I am disqualified from correcting my son. I'm not ready." I went to work, still steamed.

After a while, Bessie called my office. She said, "I think you'd better talk to him. This has to be taken care of."

"Bessie, I'm not spiritually up to talking to him."

She said, "Well, here he is," and handed him the phone.

When you have to, you can take care of anger fast. I got rid of it before my son took the phone. But when nothing forces us to deal with our anger, we tend to hang onto it. Obey the Bible. Get rid of it. Don't sleep on it.

As a Christian, anger must be put away once and for all. Do you think that is impossible? It isn't with

God. Get rid of it, and do it *now*. It is not a process. The text does not say, "Confess your sin when you get angry." It says to get rid of the anger. If you treat getting rid of anger as a process, it will never be gone. If you really can't obey this, it simply means you are not saved. The only other option is that you are *choosing* to live like a non-believer.

When you pray about your anger, don't just pray for forgiveness for the latest occurrence. Pray that God would take it away completely so that there is no real temptation. Ask Him to fill your heart up with good things. I have implemented this in my own life and seen it work.

If you hear yourself making excuses for why you are angry, just stop. Don't let yourself get away with that. Don't say, "I made a mistake." Mistake, my foot! 2 + 2 = 5. That's a mistake. Your anger is sin. God only forgives sin when you call it what it is.

Most of the Christian men I know who have an anger problem have had it for many years and have managed to keep it a secret from the church. I learn of it after it has gone on for a long time. I know I can help.

I feel so strongly about this that I urge people to never marry someone who does not have victory over anger. If the person has had major anger problems in the past, there is a high chance that after marriage it could flare up again and there will be physical violence. Domestic violence even among those who claim to follow the Lord is one of the sins that the church has often been very gifted at covering up, especially if it's a deacon, elder or even the pastor or worship leader. If you are failing a lot in this area, you need to get help. Just reading Proverbs will not be enough. You need help, which will always include repentance and walking in the light.[6]

6. Verwer, George. *More Drops.* (Secunderabad: GS Books, 2015), p. 23.

CHAPTER 9

How to Be Free from Greed and Coveting

You shall not covet your neighbor's house; you shall not covet your neighbor's wife, or his manservant or maidservant, or his ox or donkey, or anything that belongs to your neighbor. (Exod. 20:17)

When I first moved to Moscow, Idaho, I met a young divorcee with little children who came to the Bible fellowship in our home. One day, she said, "My former husband is still seeing the children, and I think he's suicidal. Would you help him? He's staying with a friend in a trailer park in Pullman."

I went to see him. He wasn't suicidal, but he had problems, so I talked with him. During our conversation, I asked why the divorce had happened.

He said, "Oh, my wife was materialistic. All she thought about was things, things, things. If she needed a can opener, she wouldn't be happy with a hand-crank can opener; she had to have an electric one. I couldn't stand the materialism of that woman."

When I saw her again, I also asked her the reason for the divorce.

"Oh," she said, "My husband was so materialistic. All he thought about was money, money, money. He's got so much money in the bank, but I could never get anything out of him. He was always trying to get more money."

They were both covetous, greedy people; they were just greedy for different things—she wanted stuff, and he wanted money.

"Put to death, therefore, whatever belongs to your earthly nature: sexual immorality, impurity, lust, evil desires and *greed, which is idolatry*" (Col. 3:5). The KJV renders this "covetousness," making greed and covetousness synonyms. Greed is inordinately desiring something that you don't have. It normally refers to the desire for money, but that is because money buys things (although some people just want the money itself). Jesus said we cannot serve God and money. One will be your God. The desire for money and things is an idol. Where your thoughts are is what you worship. "For of this you can be sure: No immoral, impure or greedy person—such a man is an idolater—has any inheritance in the kingdom of Christ and of God" (Eph. 5:5).

Sometimes what we want seems innocent, and we do not think it could possibly be sin. Wanting is not necessarily innocent. You may say, "I do not covet my neighbor's stuff, but if I did it would not be bad, because I am not stealing anything." It is still coveting. If it was his wife you were coveting, it would also be adultery.

There is a special kind of coveting that wants to have something that belongs to another person and also wants them to *not* have it. This is envy. Envy is what caused the scribes, Pharisees, and Sadducees to have Jesus murdered. If you find yourself wishing you had someone else's money, talent, looks, education, job, reputation, spouse, boyfriend, girlfriend, etc., you are envying them. You have two choices in this situation: you can keep the envy and lose your joy, or you can stop it. Confess your envy as sin. Thank God for whatever this person has that you wanted. Pray for his or her success in whatever area you are envious of.

Coveting is one of the world's favorite pastimes. This sin is rampant in the United States (although it is not limited to wealthy nations). Almost all advertising encourages it. The stores covet your money and encourage you to covet their merchandise. Of course, it is possible to purchase something without coveting it, but do not assume that purchasing it guarantees that you did not covet it first.

As Jesus started on his way, a man ran up to him and fell on his knees before him. "Good teacher," he asked, "what must I do to inherit eternal life?"

"Why do you call me good?" Jesus answered. "No one is good—except God alone. You know the commandments: 'You shall not murder, you shall not commit adultery, you shall not steal, you shall not give false testimony, you shall not defraud, honor your father and mother.'"

"Teacher," he declared, "all these I have kept since I was a boy."

Jesus looked at him and loved him. "One thing you lack," he said. "Go, sell everything you have and give to the poor, and you will have treasure in heaven. Then come, follow me."

At this the man's face fell. He went away sad, because he had great wealth.

Jesus looked around and said to his disciples, "How hard it is for the rich to enter the kingdom of God!"

The disciples were amazed at his words. But Jesus said again, "Children, how hard it is to enter the kingdom of God! *It is easier for a camel to go through the eye of a needle than for someone who is rich to enter the kingdom of God.*"

The disciples were even more amazed, and said to each other, "Who then can be saved?"

Jesus looked at them and said, "With man this is impossible, but not with God; all things are possible with God." (Mark 10:17–27)

Look at verse 26 again. "The disciples were even more amazed, and said to each other, 'Who then can be saved?'" The disciples realized that everyone was guilty. "Who then can be saved?" Jesus agreed with them. With people, it is impossible. We are all guilty.

"For of this you can be sure: No immoral, impure or *greedy* person—*such a man is an idolater*—has any inheritance in the kingdom of Christ and of God" (Eph. 5:5). The covetous man is an idolater. His inheritance is not in heaven.

"He is conceited and understands nothing. He has an unhealthy interest in controversies and quarrels about words that result in envy, strife, malicious talk, evil suspicions and constant friction between men of corrupt mind, who have been robbed of the truth and *who think that godliness is a means to financial gain.*" (1 Tim. 6:4–5). To a certain extent, everyone is materialistic, and everyone is greedy, but some people make it a virtue. There is an entire religion devoted to this, called the health and wealth gospel. Followers of the health and wealth gospel think that godliness is a means to financial gain. They say that wanting money is a good thing.

I once stopped in Kennewick, Washington, to talk to someone who is very much into this philosophy. He was wearing a T-shirt that said, "Millionaire en Route." He has a job that barely puts food on the table, but two different churches have given him prophecies that he is going to be very wealthy, and he believes them.

One of the major tenets of the Mormon Church is that godliness brings financial gain. They claim that wealth is evidence of the blessing of God on your life. Consequently, in Salt Lake City, they cheat each other all the time and say it is not cheating because God's blessing is on financial gain.

Gain is not evidence of godliness. "But *godliness with contentment* is great gain" (1 Tim. 6:6). Paul said, "I am content with anything. I have learned how to be poor, and I have learned how to be abundant." Godliness with contentment is great gain—but it is not financial gain.

"For we brought nothing into the world, and we can take nothing out of it" (1 Tim. 6:7). We come in without, and we go out without. As Billy Graham said, "I've never seen a hearse pulling a U-Haul."

"But if we have food and clothing, we will be content with that" (1 Tim. 6:8). Many people don't even have food or clothing.

"People who want to get rich fall into temptation and a trap and into many foolish and harmful desires that plunge men into ruin and destruction" (1 Tim. 6:9). *Want* and *desires*: that is where the covetousness lies. The problem is not the money; it is in the desire for it. The Scripture says, "Lead us not into temptation" (Matt. 6:13). People who want to get rich are *asking* for temptation. That temptation is a trap, and they are going to fall into it.

There are several reasons I don't play the lottery. First, I think it's greed. Second, it's wanting to get something for nothing (i.e., it's gambling). Third, I know I would win. Then I would be in big trouble. I would be embarrassed out of my mind if I won a million dollars playing the lottery. I would want to shuffle it off onto some Bible translators really fast before anyone found out I had it.

"For the love of money is a root of all kinds of evil. Some people, eager for money, have wandered from the faith and pierced themselves with many griefs" (1 Tim. 6:10). Want, desires, love, *evil.* That is what covetousness is.

How about a moderate amount? A moderate eagerness, a moderate love for money? What we think of as moderate today is a nice home with conveniences that people of my generation, when I was young, would think were filthy rich. They would wonder how you could have *so much.* We don't see it as filthy rich; we might even see it as barely making it. The important question is, "Are you content?" Someone once asked John D. Rockefeller how much money a fellow needed, and he said, "Just a little bit more." We are very seldom happy with what we have.

> For the love of money is a root of all kinds of evil. Some people, eager for money, have wandered from the faith and pierced themselves with many griefs.
>
> But you, man of God, *flee from all this, and pursue righteousness,* godliness, faith, love, endurance and gentleness. (1 Tim. 6:10–11)

> Command those who are rich in this present world
> not to be arrogant nor to put their hope in wealth,
> which is so uncertain, but to put their hope in God,
> who richly provides us with everything for our en-
> joyment. (1 Tim. 6:17)

How can we be freed from greed? *Flee* the love of money and *pursue* righteousness, godliness, faith, love, perseverance, and gentleness. Hold things in an open hand to the Lord.

I was forced to flee from the love of money almost immediately after I first experienced it. This happened a long time ago, but it taught me a lesson.

I grew up in the Depression. When I was seven, the rent for our house was fifteen dollars per month. My father worked in a packing house in Omaha making thirty dollars per month. We were poor, but we were eating, and we were content. Then my father had a car accident and lost his job. When he got out of the hospital, he had to go on welfare, so we were very poor. This went on until close to World War II, when he was able to work full-time again. In 1943, when I was fifteen, he had a massive heart attack. He couldn't work, and we were poor again. We lived on ten acres and had quite a few animals. Everything on the farm was pregnant, including my mother.

My older brother was in the Navy, which left me as the head of the house. As soon as I turned sixteen in October 1943, I got a job at the stockyards and worked from three thirty to eleven thirty every night. (I was in a soft high school—I didn't do a stitch of homework for the next two years.) I made sixty-two cents an hour, but I didn't see any of it; it was all turned over to my mother to support the family. If I got a five-cent ice cream cone once in a while, I thought it was great. But I thought that was normal, so I wasn't unhappy about it.

As soon as I was old enough, I enlisted in the Navy and supported the family from there. After a year, I got an appointment to the Naval Academy. At the Academy, they fed me, clothed me, and gave me four dollars per month spending money. My second year, I got paid seven dollars per month, the third year nine dollars, and the fourth year eleven dollars. (They gave us a bigger salary than that, but they took the rest out for uniforms and whatnot.) I wasn't able to send any money home from there since I was not allowed to work on the side, but my brother was out of the Navy at that time, so he took care of the family.

By the time I was twenty-two years old, the most money I had ever seen was eleven dollars per month. But I was always eating and was always content.

In June 1950, I graduated from the Naval Academy, was commissioned, and went directly to sea in the Korean War. We were at sea for months at a time. When we came to port, it was only to refuel and reload. I was paid about three hundred dollars per month. It might as well have been a million dollars. I was so rich! I tithed and sent a hundred dollars home to help out. There was no place to spend the rest of the money, so I started collecting it. In just a few months, I had six hundred dollars in the bank, which would be about six thousand dollars in today's currency. I thought I was rich. But I was also focused on that money. I had never been focused on money before—I hadn't had any to focus on! Now, all of a sudden, it took my attention.

One day I was in my time with the Lord—I won't say I exactly had a conversation with the Lord, but it went something like this.

The Lord said, "Wilson, I want your money."

"Lord, I'm tithing. You got Your tenth."

"I want your money."

"How much?"

"All of it."

I couldn't get away from it. I had no peace until I took the money out and sent it off to several Christian missions.

With great relief, I relaxed and said, "Boy, I'm glad that's done. Now that the Lord's paid off, I can get back to saving money."

By November, I had collected another six hundred dollars.

The voice came again: "I want your money."

"Lord," I said, "How often are You going to do this?"

"How long will it take you to learn?"

I checked out the six hundred dollars, but I didn't know where to give it, so I kept it in the safe in my stateroom.

After my ship hit a mine, we spent a month in dry dock in Sasebo, Japan. Then the ship went on to Yokosuka. From Yokosuka, I caught a train to Tokyo to have lunch with a missionary friend named David Morken. At lunch, David introduced me to the man who had been the youngest Olympic runner in the 1936 games in Berlin when he was eighteen years old. He became famous by tearing down the swastika at the Third Reich headquarters in Berlin. He was later shot down in the Pacific, spent forty-seven days on a life raft, was strafed by Japanese planes, and was finally captured when his raft washed ashore. When they found out he was an Olympic athlete, they made him run against Japanese athletes when he was starving. He came back to the U.S. after the war and was converted in Billy Graham's first evangelistic crusade in Los Angeles in 1949. When I met him, he had been a Christian for about a year and had returned to Japan to witness to the guards who had held him captive and to tell them that he had forgiven them because he had been forgiven. His name was Lou Zamperini.[7]

During the lunch, Lou said that he was in trouble. His home in North Hollywood was going to be foreclosed, and he had no money.

I asked him how much he needed.

He said, "Six hundred dollars."

7. Author of *Devil at My Heels* and subject of the World War II biography *Unbroken* by Laura Hillenbrand.

"Come with me." We caught a train to Yokosuka and went aboard the ship. I opened the safe and gave him the six hundred dollars cash.

He said, "This is a loan," and wrote an IOU on a three-by-five card.

I said, "No, it's not." I knew it was a gift, so I paid no attention to the card. In fact, I kept telephone numbers on it, and accidentally left it in a telephone booth in Tokyo. David Morken found it and returned it to me.

Lou wrote later to pay me back. I said the money wasn't mine and told him to give it to missions instead.

If you give a tenth to the Lord and think the other ninety percent is yours, you're crazy. The tenth off the top is the Lord's, but the rest is also the Lord's, because you are committed to Him. That second time, I learned my lesson. It took away my covetousness for years.

God taught me that lesson, and He taught me well. That was the beginning of my fleeing from the love of money. The real solution to my being free from the love of money since then has been pursuing righteousness, godliness, faith, love, patience, and gentleness. Make a one-time decision by the grace of God to forsake the love of money, then begin to pursue good things.

After Bessie and I were married, I had two other bouts of covetousness. The first was in 1961. We had four children. We were very poor and lived in a cheap rental house. I suddenly wanted to own a house. I wanted one that was big enough, with a garden, a small orchard, and a white picket fence. Bessie was in the hospital for two weeks. While she was there, I filled the time wandering around looking at houses with orchards and gardens and white picket fences. I was miserable. I wanted a nice house. I wanted to be rich.

Then I realized it had been the most miserable two weeks of my life. "Those who want to get rich fall into temptation and a trap and into many foolish and harmful desires that plunge people into ruin and destruction" (1 Tim. 6:9). I became very conscious of my sin. I confessed it, quit looking for a house, and my joy returned. Before the year was over after confessing my sin, a house was given to me. It is an amazing story.

God has provided for our needs, and we can honestly say that we are not attached to money at all. But it was painful getting unattached. It's like breaking up with a girlfriend. When you are attached to something, it hurts to break up. We are not allowed to be attached.

Coveting does not end at longing for things that do not belong to you. You can also covet your own possessions.

> Someone in the crowd said to him, "Teacher, tell my brother to divide the inheritance with me." Jesus replied, "Man, who appointed me a judge or an arbiter between you?" Then he said to them, "Watch out! Be on your guard against all kinds of greed; life does not consist in an abundance of possessions." And he told them this parable: "The ground of a certain rich man yielded an abundant harvest. He thought to himself,

'What shall I do? I have no place to store my crops.' Then he said, 'This is what I'll do. I will tear down my barns and build bigger ones, and there I will store my surplus grain. And I'll say to myself, "You have plenty of grain laid up for many years. Take life easy; eat, drink and be merry."' But God said to him, 'You fool! This very night your life will be demanded from you. Then who will get what you have prepared for yourself?' This is how it will be with whoever stores up things for themselves but is not rich toward God."
(Luke 12:13–21)

In my second-class year at the Naval Academy, I received my class ring. It was so heavy that I would go to bed with my arm hanging over the side. Only a small minority of naval officers are Academy graduates. Consequently, there is a certain amount of envy among the other officers. At meal times, we all stood behind our chairs until the captain came in and sat down. The chairs were metal. When we grasped the backs of the chairs, our heavy rings would ring out against the metal. Therefore, Academy men were known as "ring knockers."

In the spring of 1953, my ship stopped over in Pearl Harbor. Since the submarine base had the best officers' club, we went over there to use the swimming pool. While swimming, I lost my ring. We swam around the bottom of the pool looking for it but did not find it. I left a note at the club but never heard from them.

I did not consider the ring as being a thing I coveted—until I lost it. I was sick about it for several weeks. Then I realized that it was an idol in my life. I confessed the sin and thanked God that the ring was gone. My joy returned.

Five years later, I was out of the Navy and in Christian work. I received a telephone call from the Bureau of Naval Personnel. The voice said for me to come down to the office to pick up my ring. The class year, '50, had been filed off. Someone had been pretending to be a ring knocker during those five years.

God chastens us to bring sin to our attention. He does this so that we will confess and be forgiven. Psalm 39 tells of a certain type of chastening.

> And now, Lord, for what do I wait?
>> My hope is in thee.
> Deliver me from all my transgressions . . . .
>
> Remove thy stroke from me;
>> I am spent by the blows of thy hand.
> When thou dost chasten man
>> with rebukes for sin,
> thou dost consume like a moth what is dear to him;
>> surely every man is a mere breath! *Selah*
> (Psalm 39:7–8a, 10–11 RSV)

Have you ever had something that you were inordinately fond of, something that was so precious to you that you could not let it go? Then you sinned, and the Lord took away your plaything. The thing you loved may or may not have been related to the sin, although your inordinate affection for it could have been sin in itself. God needed to get your attention, so He took it. He consumes like a moth what is dear to you—just eats it up!

If you don't want the Lord consuming like a moth what is dear to you, 1) don't get into sin, and 2) don't let anything be inordinately precious to you. If something is too dear to you, you are asking for trouble. Everything we have should be held in an open hand to the Lord. If you are hanging on to it and you don't dare let go, that is covetousness. This includes things that are perfectly legitimate to have, like your wife or your husband. They are the Lord's gift to you. But if that person or that thing becomes more important to you than God, He might get your attention by taking it away. (I don't think the Psalm is specifically speaking of people, but it can include that.) It could be your house. It could be your car. It could be the sterling silver. It could be a set of china. It could be the bushes in the front yard. It could be anything.

It could be money. This was the problem of the divorced couple I mentioned earlier. They were both afflicted with the same problem. Both had something inordinately dear to them: he was greedy for money, and she was greedy for things. Of course they couldn't live together! The inordinate dearness of things and money was more important to each of them than the other person was.

The missionary Barclay Buxton[8] was sitting in his garden one day talking with a friend while his boys played rugby on the lawn. One tackled another, and they accidentally smashed a bush. Barclay Buxton didn't say anything.

His friend said, "Barclay, aren't you going to speak to your boys about what they're doing to the garden?"

"Sir," he said, "I'm raising boys, not bushes."

Where is your value?

William Pape, a missionary and a dear friend of mine, went to the Lisu people in Southwest China before World War II. All his worldly belongings were packed for the trip there in seven trunks. As they were getting into the mountains, they passed through a village that had just been raided by bandits. Word reached them that the bandits were running rampant along the trail, looting and taking everything.

Bill began to worry about his trunks. Suppose the bandits took them? Everything he possessed was inside them. How was he going to be a missionary in the mountains without those trunks? He was terribly anxious for miles and miles and days and days.

Finally, he said, "Lord, I wish those bandits would hurry up and get these trunks! As long as I have them, they are an anxiety to me." As soon as he turned them

---

8. One of the founders of the Japan Evangelistic Band.

over to the Lord (or to the bandits, whoever wanted them), he was free.

The bandits did not get his trunks. Years later, the Japanese did get them. Then Bill said, "I suddenly realized what freedom it was to have a Bible and a toothbrush, to not be attached to things."

God wants us to be attached to Him. "Surely man goes about as a shadow! Surely for nought are they in turmoil; man heaps up, and knows not who will gather!" (Psalm 39:6 RSV). When you die, you don't know who's going to get it. God does not hold things in very high importance. He says that we shouldn't, either.

Jim Elliott, one of the missionaries killed by the Auca Indians in 1956, wrote in his diary, "He is no fool who gives what he cannot keep to gain what he cannot lose." He did that. He gave his life (he couldn't keep it) to gain an everlasting crown. It is not foolish to give what you cannot keep to gain what you cannot lose. Give your possessions; you cannot keep them anyhow. Give your life; you cannot keep it anyhow.

What about things you cannot literally give up, like grades in school? How do you do that? The answer goes back to why you are in school in the first place. Are you in school to get an education, to learn, or are you in school for the grades?

Suppose there are two music majors in college. One practices because he has to in order to get a high grade. The other practices because he loves music so much. He wants to. He has also given his music over to the

Lord, so he plays for the glory of God. His motivation is directly in line with his objective (to be a musician); his desire is the same as the end.

Who will be the better musician—the one who practices because he enjoys music and is doing it for the glory of God, or the one who practices because if he doesn't he will flunk and have to explain to his parents?

Look at where you are and say, "Why am I here?" Colossians 3:23 helped me here. "And whatever you do, do it heartily, as to the Lord and not to men, knowing that from the Lord you will receive the reward of the inheritance; for you serve the Lord Christ" (Col. 3:23–24 NKJV). If God has called me to be a student, He wants me to study heartily, but for Him, not for the grades. If I do school heartily for the Lord, I will probably get grades that are just as good as—or even better than—if I were doing it just for the grades. Take where you are and say, "I am going to do this for the Lord."

What if you can't do it for God? Then maybe you should not be doing what you are doing. Perhaps you are in the wrong field.

This is what kept me going in the Navy for so long. I had to determine whether I was going to do it for my glory, do it for the captain, or do it for God. The only way I could stay sane was to do it for God. I would have wiped out if I had tried to do it any other way.

It is not enough to be convicted, to go around feeling rotten about the possessions that you don't want to let go of. You have to fish or cut bait. You can't sit around and do nothing. Do not procrastinate. Right now, just say, "Lord, you can have all of me and all of my possessions."

If you are not up to doing that, think of the one thing that you are too attached to. Say, "Lord, I want to give it to You before You take it away." It won't hurt as much if you give it up first.

Spend some time in prayer. Take the thing that you are holding in a grasped hand and let go of it. Tell God it's His if He wants it. Preferably, do that with your whole life—not only about whether you live or die, but why you're living. "Lord, it's Yours, and everything that is attached to me."

When you make a complete surrender like this, it is a good thing to think in terms of specifics so that you know what constitutes the whole. You can't possibly mention everything, but you should have some comprehension of what you mean when you tell the Lord He can have "all of it."

For example, when I was preparing to leave the Navy for full-time Christian work, I told the Lord that I was willing to go anyplace in the world as a missionary. I picked the most absurd locations: Port Lyautey, North Africa, Antarctica, etc. I told Him I would go anywhere for Him.

The Lord came back and said, "Fine. Stay in the Navy."

I said, "Lord! I meant anyplace *else!*" I thought I was willing to go anywhere as a missionary, but it didn't occur to me to include the Navy in my thinking, so it was a big shock to find out that I had really meant anyplace *else*. Include specifics in your thinking, including the specific of where you are right now.

You may not be able to make this surrender. If you are not, there might be sin in the way. Before you make the surrender, do some confessing.

If you are not sure whether you are a Christian, and you make this complete surrender to the Lord ("Lord, You can have me and do whatever You want with me."), when you finish praying, you will be a Christian, because that is how you become one. You surrender, and the Lord does the changing.

Sometimes we think that holding something in an open hand to the Lord means that we have to get rid of it. I don't think that's true, although it might be. If God knows you can't be trusted, He might want you to give it away, as He did with me and the six hundred dollars. Sometimes the Lord literally takes it. But it is better for you to give it than for Him to consume it.

When we were living in Japan after we were married, I would not usually take my lunch to work with me; I would eat with the bachelor officers in the officers' club in order to witness to them. One particular day, I was eating lunch in the club with a group of officers who were cutting a wide swath of immorality in Japan. I was friends with them and loving them.

For dessert, I ordered a hot fudge sundae. I was digging into it when Sam Driver said, "Jim, we don't think you should eat that hot fudge sundae."

I said, "Why not?"

"We've been watching you for a long time. We've come to the conclusion that in your books, if it's pleasant, it's sin. You're obviously enjoying that hot fudge sundae, and we don't want you in sin."

I said, "You've missed it completely. 1 Timothy 6:17 says, 'Command those who are rich in this present age not to be haughty, nor to trust in uncertain riches but in the living God, who gives us richly all things to enjoy.'"

It is possible to be a Christian and be rich in this present world. The problem is not being rich; the problem is being eager to be rich. God richly provides us with all things for our enjoyment. God is not opposed to enjoyment. He gave us ears for music, and we can hear the finest sounds in a symphony. He gave us color and eyes to interpret it. He gave us richly all things to enjoy. He simply enjoins us not to trust in the things He gives us, but in Him.

I quoted that verse to Sam and said, "God gave this sundae to me. I've already thanked Him for it, and I'm enjoying it." God is not opposed to the enjoyment of things; He is just opposed to enjoyment of them as an *end*.

"I know what it is to be in need, and I know what it is to have plenty. I have learned the secret of being content in any and every situation, whether well fed or hungry, whether living in plenty or in want. I can do all this through him who gives me strength" (Phil. 4:12–13 NKJV).

CHAPTER 10

How to Be Free from Stealing

Whoever can be trusted with very little can also be
trusted with much, and whoever is dishonest with
very little will also be dishonest with much. So if
you have not been trustworthy in handling worldly wealth, who will trust you with true riches? And if
you have not been trustworthy with someone else's
property, who will give you property of your own?
(Luke 16:10–12)

Stealing is a common characteristic of the unsaved
man. It is sin (Exod. 20:15), and in most countries it is
also a crime. If we think of it as crime, we can be grate-
ful that we have not been caught. If we think of it as sin,
we know that we are *always* caught.

Most stealing is not robbery or shoplifting. It is being dishonest in very little or being dishonest in much. As a crime, this kind of stealing is divided into two categories: petty larceny (a misdemeanor) and grand larceny (a felony). Sin is also measured in size; however, the size of the theft does not affect the penalty. The wages of sin is death.

If you are a normal, moral person, that is, not into drugs, sex, or alcohol, you are probably still guilty of stealing.

> The LORD said to Moses: "If anyone sins and is unfaithful to the LORD by deceiving his neighbor about something entrusted to him or left in his care or stolen, or if he cheats him, or if he finds lost property and lies about it, or if he swears falsely, or if he commits any such sin that people may do—when he thus sins and becomes guilty, he must *return what he has stolen* or taken by extortion, or what was entrusted to him, or the lost property he found, or whatever it was they swore falsely about. He must *make restitution in full, add a fifth of the value to it and give it all to the owner* on the day he presents his guilt offering. And as a penalty he must bring to the priest, that is, to the LORD, his guilt offering, a ram from the flock, one without defect and of the proper value. In this way the priest will make atonement for him before the LORD, and they will be forgiven for any of the things he did that made him guilty." (Lev. 6:1–7)

The solution to stealing is confession of the theft and either returning the stolen goods or making payment for them plus twenty percent of their value.

Very small sin leads to great sin. It is naïve to think the dishonesty seen in the scandals that break around us started out with big sin. If what Jesus said in Luke 16 is true, the guilty ones were dishonest in the little things first.

Stealing is one sin people don't like to talk about. That could indicate that stealing is very rare—or the opposite, that it is frequent, but we hide it. Why? We do not want to return what we stole, or we do not want family members or friends to know that we stole from them. Unless you take care of this, your stealing will probably continue. You cannot be free from future stealing until all past stealing is forgiven.

I am assuming that everyone has stolen in the past. I do not know for sure that this is true, but I suspect it is. Over the past five years, about five million people have been *caught* shoplifting in the United States. But the National Association for Shoplifting Prevention estimates that the actual number of shoplifters in the country is much higher—approximately twenty-seven million.[9]

I was no exception to this. When I was in first grade, there was a corner grocery store at 24th and Oak, about

9. "Shoplifting Statistics," National Association for Shoplifting Prevention, accessed October 29, 2018, http://www.shopliftingprevention. org/what-we-do/learning-resource-center/statistics.

two blocks from home. One day after school, I was walking home past the corner grocery with my friend Ralph when he volunteered to teach me how to steal a cookie.

I was interested. Ralph's mother had given him money to buy a pound of hamburger. He told me, "When I order the hamburger, the owner will go to the back room to grind and wrap it. While he is back there, we go over to the cookie bin, open the glass lid, take out two cookies, and put them in our pockets." He would pay the merchant for the hamburger, and we would leave the store.

It worked like a charm. While the owner was out of sight, Ralph zipped over to the cookie bin, took two cookies, and slipped one to me. He paid, and we continued our walk home.

The cookies had a marshmallow on top and were dipped in chocolate. I ate mine in the first block. Then I realized that Mom would see the chocolate on my face and make inquiries about where I got it. I spent the second block industriously licking and scrubbing at my face to remove the evidence. She never asked.

Fifteen years later during my second year at the U.S. Naval Academy, I received Christ. While on leave the following year, I went back to 24th and Oak Street in South Omaha to make restitution for the stolen cookie. The store was no longer there, so I gave the money to the Lord.

I do not know how many people steal from their parents or in their tax returns or by not paying student loans, but I assume the number is high. Leviticus 6 also includes lost property that you have found and kept as stealing. If you find something and think, "Finders keepers," that is a false justification for keeping something that belongs to someone else.

One Sunday, I was preaching on the subject of taking back what you've stolen. After the service, a young man asked to see me urgently. I told him it was not possible, and he would have to come to my home that afternoon.

He came with his wife. They were very young (perhaps nineteen and twenty). He was a student at the local university. I asked him why he wanted to see me. He said that it was about what I had preached that morning.

"Wasn't it clear?"

Student: "Yes."

"Then why do you need to see me? You know what to do."

Student: "Let me tell you anyway. I stole seventy rock music tapes that cost $6.99 each from a music store. I don't like that kind of music anymore, so I threw them away. I have a leather fringe coat that I don't wear because it bothers my conscience. I have a pair of running shoes I found at the boat races in the Tri-Cities. I have a basketball from the men's gym, and I stole a bike ten years ago in Spokane."

"What is your problem? You know what to do."

Student: "I don't have any money."

"What are you and your wife living on?"

Student: "All the money I earned last summer. I have it budgeted out for the school year."

"Oh," I said, "You *do* have money. Except it's not your money. It belongs to the people you stole from."

Later he told me the success of the restitution. He went to the house in Spokane where he had taken the bicycle. When he knocked on the door, a man answered. He asked the man if he had lost a bike ten years ago. He said he didn't know, and he would ask his wife. His wife said they had. He gave her the money for the bike. She took it and went over to the corner of the room to count it. He made similar restitution for the rest of the stolen goods.

Another student had been a heavy-equipment driver for a construction company. At the beginning of the summer, he told his boss that he planned on going back to college in the fall. When he came to work the next day, the boss told him, "Since you are leaving in the fall, just don't come back tomorrow."

The student was angry that the boss had only given him one day's notice when he had given the boss three months' notice. He figured that the company owed him something, so he took a few tools with him when he left that day.

In the fall, he heard the message on restitution and realized he had to return the tools. At Christmas, he put the tools in his car. While driving to the construction company, he was listening to Christian radio. The Bible teacher on the radio said that restitution was an Old Testament concept and that people under grace did not have to return things.

He was so glad! He turned around, went home, and engraved his initials on the tools. Later he was again convicted by the Holy Spirit. This time he had to take the tools back with his initials on them.

Restitution is for people under grace. Here's why.

> The LORD said to Moses, "Say to the Israelites: 'Any man or woman wrongs another in any way and so is unfaithful to the LORD, that person is guilty and must confess the sin he has committed. He must make full restitution for his wrong, add one fifth to it and give it all to the person he has wronged. But if that person has no close relative to whom restitution can be made for the wrong, the restitution belongs to the LORD and must be given to the priest, along with the ram with which atonement is made for him." (Num. 5:6–8)

In the Old Testament, two things were required to absolve your guilt when you had stolen something. They were 1) a sacrifice and 2) restitution.

God provided forgiveness of sins in the death and resurrection of Jesus Christ. He is the sacrifice prefigured in Leviticus 6:6 ("And as a penalty he must bring to the priest, that is, to the LORD, his guilt offering, a ram from the flock, one without defect and of the proper value.") and realized in Hebrews 10:10 ("And by that will, we have been made holy through the sacrifice of the body of Jesus Christ once for all.").

Jesus's death on the cross is the fulfillment of all the Old Testament sacrifices: "Unlike the other high priests, he does not need to offer sacrifices day after day, first for his own sins, and then for the sins of the people. He sacrificed for their sins once for all when he offered himself" (Heb. 7:27). Jesus does not repay the man who got ripped off. You are supposed to do that.

Look at the restitution in the story of Jesus's encounter with Zacchaeus in Luke 19: "But Zacchaeus stood up and said to the Lord, 'Look, Lord! Here and now I give half of my possessions to the poor, and if I have cheated anybody out of anything, I will pay back four times the amount.' Jesus said to him, 'Today salvation has come to this house, because this man, too, is a son of Abraham'" (Luke 19:8–9). Zacchaeus returned fourfold to the people he had cheated.

Restitution is repentance in action. Repentance that hangs on to the money is not repentance. You can plead that the batteries shoplifted from the drugstore in junior high were taken ten years before your conversion, and that conversion was five years ago. That makes no difference. The batteries were not yours then, and they are not yours now. Even though you were truly forgiven for stealing them when you turned to Christ, if you choose not to pay for the batteries, you are in effect stealing them again.

John the Baptist and Paul each made strong statements about this. John: "Produce fruit in keeping with repentance" (Matt. 3:8). Paul: "I preached that they should repent and turn to God and *prove their repentance by their deeds*" (Acts 26:20).

Once there was a man who robbed a bank. The result was a hundred thousand dollars in his briefcase. Five minutes later, he was walking down the street, briefcase in hand, when he encountered an evangelistic street meeting. He stopped to listen to the gospel and was convicted and converted. In his new-found joy, he went up to talk to the evangelist.

"I did what you said. I prayed to God. I feel wonderful! What does that mean?"

The preacher said, "That means you have been born again."

"What does that mean?"

"It means your sins have been forgiven."

"All of them?" asked the man.

"Yes, all of them," answered the evangelist.

"Oh boy," he replied. "Now I can enjoy this hundred thousand dollars."

"What hundred thousand dollars?"

"In my briefcase. I just relieved the bank of some extra money."

The preacher looked at him. "Let's take it back."

Being forgiven does not mean you get to keep the money. You may think that is so obvious it doesn't need to be taught. There are two reasons it is obvious in this story: 1) It was one hundred thousand dollars, not five bucks. 2) It was ten minutes ago (and before his conversion), not twenty years ago.

Suppose, however, it was five dollars twenty years before your conversion. Is the principle still just as clear? If not, where is the cutoff point, either in the size of the theft or in the amount of time since it occurred? Is restitution required only in big and recent things?

No matter the amount (large or tiny), no matter how long ago it was (five minutes or fifty years), it is not your money. You can confess the theft and be forgiven for stealing it, but if you decide to keep it, you have just stolen it again.

But what if it is a candy bar you took twenty years ago? The amount stolen and the time since the theft do *not* make it *yours*. Take it back!

I have had people object to returning stolen property because the amount was in the thousands of dollars, and they did not have the money and could not foresee ever having it. Others object because it was only a small amount of money, and, consequently, it did not matter. The objections go on and on.

Some people have forgotten which stores they shoplifted from, or the stores have closed, or the people they stole from have died. Numbers 5:8 has a solution for this. "But if that person has no close relative to whom restitution can be made for the wrong, the restitution belongs to the LORD and must be given to the priest, along with the ram with which atonement is made for him." If the money cannot be returned to the original owner, give it to the Lord. You may not keep it.

It is not yours. If you don't remember how much you took, make a high estimate and add twenty percent.

Countless Christians are living subnormal Christian lives because they are too proud or too afraid to make restitution. Their spiritual life has a low-grade fever—not sick enough to be in bed, but too sick to do anything worthwhile. Even if no one knows about the thefts, these Christians are poor witnesses for Jesus Christ. They may have confessed and repented in words, but if they do not make restitution, it is not true repentance, and they are not forgiven. You must *confess* the theft and *return* what you stole before you can be set free from stealing.

How do you prevent it from happening again? One preventative is to *confess coveting*. Another is to *be content with what you have*. A man's life does not consist of the abundance of his possessions. If there is something you need or think you need, save up for it, work for it, or live without it.

Many years ago, a woman came in to the bookstore to see me. She was suicidal. I gave her advice and told her that she would have to do what I said, or I would not see her again. I saw her several times, and she really improved.

One day, I noticed that she talked about *things* a lot. It sounded like coveting. I thought about that. It did not seem that should could be that covetous without stealing. I immediately told her that I wanted a list of all the places she had stolen from with an estimate of the dollar value of the items stolen.

She tried to say that she did not steal—she might have taken home a few sheets of drawing paper for her kids, but that was all. I told her that was not true, and I wanted the list the next week.

She came in with a list of stores and a total of about eight hundred dollars. The following week, she brought four hundred dollars, which I returned to the stores on the list. The week after, she gave me another four hundred dollars for the rest of the stores.

You may be stealing because of covetousness or because of other, unrelated sins that you have not confessed. If you are not in fellowship with God, Satan can tempt you to steal. In order to escape this, you must confess the other sins.

"He who has been stealing must steal no longer, but must work, doing something useful with his own hands, that he may have something to share with those in need" (Eph. 4:28).

CHAPTER 11

How to Be Free from Gossip

A perverse man stirs up dissension,
and a gossip separates close friends. (Prov. 16:28)

*G*ossip is America's favorite pastime. When we get together with our friends, the subject of our conversation is generally other people. This creates great potential for gossip.

In the early 1900s, all the telephones in the countryside were party lines. When one farmer's wife called another, all the wives on the line could pick up their phones and listen in. Today, blogs, Facebook, and other social media platforms spread gossip like wildfire.

What exactly is gossip? Gossip is vicarious enjoyment of someone else's wrongdoing (or supposed wrongdoing, failures, etc.)—savoring it by talking about the sin and listening to others talk about it. And since so many enjoy both receiving and passing on gossip, it spreads far and wide quickly. Gossip is like taking a down pillow to the top of a windy hill, slicing it open, and shaking the feathers into the breeze. Want to deal with gossip after the fact? Try picking all that up and putting it back in the pillowcase. Good luck.

> Without wood a fire goes out;
>> without a gossip a quarrel dies down. (Prov. 26:20)

> For I am afraid that when I come I may not find you as I want you to be, and you may not find me as you want me to be. I fear that there may be discord, jealousy, fits of rage, selfish ambition, slander, gossip, arrogance and disorder. (2 Cor. 12:20)

Gossip is sharing negative information about someone who is not present. Gossip is not innocent chit-chat. It is a gross sin. It is sin even if what you are saying is *true*. You are not saying it *to* them. You are saying it behind their back, and you are not saying it to help them.

"The words of a gossip are like choice morsels; they go down to a man's inmost parts" (Prov. 18:8). Listening to gossip is as bad as talking gossip. It is great sin.

"A gossip betrays a confidence; so avoid a man who talks too much" (Prov. 20:19). What do you do when you are on the receiving end of gossip? I hear a lot of gossip while counseling people. Sometimes it is from people who come to me hoping I can do something about it. In that case, I go to the person whom the gossip is about. If I find that it is false, I try to stop it. That is very seldom successful. If I find that the gossip is true, I try to help the person with the problem.

If you realize you are about to hear gossip, ask the teller three questions: 1) Is it negative information? 2) Is it firsthand information? 3) Have you already gone to the person whom it is about? If they cannot answer these satisfactorily, inform them that you do not want to hear the gossip. If you listen to it, you are part of the gossip chain.

My wife Bessie and I found out long ago that we were not in the local gossip circuit. People could be in great trouble, and we would never hear about it. Everyone else knew because it was part of their entertainment.

We were out of the circuit for a reason. When Bessie and I had been married about six years, we moved to a new town and joined an evangelical church. We had barely gotten settled in when Bessie received a call from another woman in the church. She had a juicy bit of information about someone else in the congregation and was eager to share it.

Bessie asked, "Is that true?"

"Yes, it's true," the lady replied.

Bessie took action. "OK. Meet me over here, and you and I will go speak to her about this right now."

"What?! If you go see her, don't tell her I told you!"

Pretty soon, Bessie didn't get any telephone calls.

Her reply did not stop the gossip, but it did get her out of the mix. Normally, I am also left out of the loop. People who gossip to me know that I will tell them to go to the person directly. They also know that *I know* that they are not going to do that. They come to me, not so that I can pass it on, but so that I will seek out the truth and take biblical action. They should do this themselves.

Bessie and I were friends with a U.S. Air Force Chaplain named Augie Kilpatrick. He and his family stayed in our home for a few days while we were out of town. On one occasion, Bessie asked Augie how he handled gossip. He had a ready answer.

"I take out my pocket notebook and write down word-for-word what I am being told. After I have taken it all down, I read it back to the gossiper and ask him if it is correct and if it is true. When he says yes, I hand him the notebook and my pen and say, 'Good. Please sign here.'"

If you are going to listen to gossip, you have two options:

- Listen to the gossip and write it down word for word. Read it back to the gossiper. Ask them, "Is this true?" If the gossiper doesn't know if it's true, ask why they repeated it. If the gossiper says it is true, ask them to sign their name under your transcript.

- Listen to the gossip. Ask if it's true. Then say, "Let's go and correct this person together about this awful thing you say they did."

Your only other option is to *walk away*. Don't listen. "A gossip betrays a confidence, but a trustworthy man keeps a secret" (Prov. 11:13). "I can keep a secret. It's the people I tell it to who can't." If you don't listen to it in the first place, you can't pass it on.

Do not promise not to pass something on. I hardly ever promise to keep a confidence before I hear the story. I may promise to keep a confidence *afterward*, in which case I do keep it. However, I determine which ones I keep; the people who share them with me do not get to make that determination beforehand. This lack of promise on my part is not the same as gossip, although it could be gossip if I did not keep something that I should have kept.

The Bible requires us to tell the assembly of believers if someone is unrepentant. The believers are to take action on the unrepentant person (Matt. 18). If I have promised to keep the information secret, I have hobbled myself so that I cannot obey God by telling the church.

Many years ago, a young Christian woman on the east coast sent a friend in to my bookstore to see me. He came to Christ through a testimony in a booklet I gave him, and they were married.

Several months later, she fell in love with her lawyer boss. Bessie and I did everything we could think of to stop their relationship. We ran out of ideas. In bed that night, we asked God to do something.

The very next day, the lawyer came to see me. He wanted to tell me something about the husband, but first he wanted me to promise to keep it confidential. I told him that I did not make those kinds of promises.

He was astounded. "You are a Christian, and you don't keep confidences?" I was a minister of the gospel—I had to keep confidences!

I agreed. "Oh, I keep them. I just do not *promise* to keep them." I also told him that I determined which ones I kept after I heard the story.

"Then I can't tell you," he said.

"That's fine. I don't need to know."

He kept asking me to promise, and I kept refusing. Each time I refused, he got angrier. Finally, in hysterical fury, he left my office, slamming the door behind him. He stormed back to his law firm and told his secretary what an idiot I was.

That opened her eyes about his character. She knew I was not an idiot. My refusal to listen to his gossip ended their relationship.

Gossip has no place in the Christian life. If someone is determined to gossip with you, draw their attention to Romans 1 and 1 Corinthians 12:

They have become filled with every kind of wickedness, evil, greed and depravity. They are full of envy, murder, strife, deceit and malice. They are *gossips*,

slanderers, God-haters, insolent, arrogant and boastful; they invent ways of doing evil; they disobey their
parents; they are senseless, faithless, heartless, ruthless. *Although they know God's righteous decree that
those who do such things deserve death, they not only
continue to do these very things but also approve of
those who practice them.* (Rom. 1:29–32)

For I am afraid that when I come I may not find you
as I want you to be, and you may not find me as you
want me to be. I fear that there may be quarreling,
jealousy, outbursts of anger, factions, slander, gossip, arrogance and disorder. (2 Cor. 12:20)

Doing these things will have three effects: Some
people will quit gossiping; some will start gossiping
about you; and you will be left out of the gossip circuit.

BRIDLING THE TONGUE[10]

Some time ago, a magnetic storm occurred in New York
state that caused a conversation on a telephone line to
interfere with the radio waves emitted from a nearby
radio station. As a result, the conversation was broad-
cast on the radio without the knowledge of the two
talkers. It was a coast-to-coast program!

All of us at one time or another have been guilty of
gossip. In fact, there is enough gossip in many a church

10.   Chris Vlachos ran one of our bookstores for many years. This
section is his thoughts on gossip, excerpted from *How to Be Free
from Bitterness* and edited for this book.

to make the recording angel weep as he records it. It is a sinful practice which God takes seriously and wants us to stop.

Paul speaks of gossip in 1 Timothy 3:11 (NASB): "Women must likewise be dignified, not malicious gossips, but temperate, faithful in all things." Lest we think that men are immune to this disease, Paul similarly addresses them in his second letter to Timothy, predicting that in the last days men will be "unloving, irreconcilable, malicious gossips, without self-control, brutal, haters of good" (2 Tim. 3:3 NASB).

The Greek word which Paul uses in these two instances is *diabolos*, from which we derive our word *devil*. We don't need to consult our calendar of saints to know who the patron saint of gossip is! A gossiper is nothing more than "the devil's mailman."

Diabolos is also translated "slanderer." Gossip is slander. In the passage quoted above from 2 Timothy, Paul places gossip in the middle of a list of other vicious practices. Clearly, the serious nature of gossip is indicated.

Unfortunately, it is often difficult to recognize gossip and slander in our own speech. How can we know if we are gossips? Here are four questions to ask ourselves when we are tempted to share information concerning someone else:

1. *Why am I saying this?* Is my real motive to criticize? Am I really out to help the person about whom I am speaking, or is my goal to hurt them? Often under

the guise of sharing a prayer request we are really gossiping. We rationalize it, but our real aim is to put the other person down in order to cast ourselves in a better light. Be careful how you answer this first question. If you catch yourself trying to excuse something negative that you are about to say concerning someone, you are probably on the threshold of slander.

2. *Is it possible there is another side to the story?* Webster defines gossip as "spreading rumors." A rumor is an unauthenticated story. If we have not authenticated the story ourselves, we are gossiping. It has been said that it isn't the people who tell all they know that cause most of the trouble in the church; it is the ones who tell more than they know.

3. *Would I feel comfortable saying this to Jesus?* How would He answer you after you shared this negative information with Him? Very likely, He would respond by asking us what relevance that has to our following Him (John 21:22). If you wouldn't be comfortable sharing the tale with the Lord, then it is probably unsuitable to share with anyone else.

4. *Am I building up the person I'm speaking to by sharing this?* Charles Spurgeon once said that gossip "emits a threefold poison; it injures the teller, the hearer, and the person concerning whom the tale is told."[11] We should be very careful to heed Paul's exhortation:

11. Charles Spurgeon, *Morning by Morning*, November 29.

"Do not let any unwholesome talk come out of your mouths, but only what is helpful for building others up according to their needs, that it may benefit those who listen" (Eph. 4:29).

If after asking these four questions, you are still not sure if what you about to share is gossip, then don't say it. Is it really necessary that you do?

One last thought: How can we stop this sinful habit of gossiping that has invaded the church? The cure for gossip is twofold. First, don't spread it. Bridle your tongue! If you can't say anything good about somebody, then don't say anything at all. Second, don't listen to it! You can't have gossiping tongues unless there are gossiping ears. Don't encourage the gossiper. Don't be quick to believe what is said. Steer the conversation to a discussion of the person's *good* points. Nothing will stop a gossiper faster than doing that.

"Finally, brothers, whatever is true, whatever is noble, whatever is right, whatever is pure, whatever is lovely, whatever is admirable—if anything is excellent or praiseworthy—think about such things" (Phil. 4:8).

CONCLUSION

Any time you are part of a gossip circuit, you must call it sin, regardless of your reason for being there. You must confess it to God and receive forgiveness. Do not say it was not gossip. Treat it as gross immorality. Remember Romans 1: "They have become filled with

every kind of wickedness, evil, greed and depravity....
They are *gossips*, slanderers, God-haters, insolent, arrogant and boastful; they invent ways of doing evil . . ."
(Rom. 1:29–30). Gossips are in the list with murderers and God-haters.

"Although they know God's righteous decree that those who do such things deserve death, they not only continue to do these very things but also approve of those who practice them" (Rom. 1:32). When you gossip, you are *approving* of their sin. Your speech may have the tone and content of disapproval, but that makes no difference. You think that you are innocent because you are not, yourself, doing the sin, and you are voicing disapproval. Enjoying sin this way is sin. "For it is shameful even to mention what the disobedient do in secret" (Eph. 5:12).

CHAPTER 12

How to Be Free from Lying

Jesus said, "I am the way, the truth and the life. No man comes unto the Father but by me." (John 14:6)

And you will know the truth, and the truth will make you free. (John 8:32)

*S*peaking the truth involves more than simply passing on correct information. "If I have the gift of prophecy and can fathom all mysteries and all knowledge, and if I have a faith that can move mountains, but do not have love, I am nothing" (1 Cor. 13:2).

Truth-telling alone is not the opposite of lying. We are to speak the truth *in love* (Eph. 4:15). What is love? "Love is patient, love is kind. It does not envy, it does not boast, it is not proud. It is not rude, it is not self-seeking, it is not easily angered, it keeps no record of wrongs. Love does not delight in evil but rejoices with the truth. It always protects, always trusts, always hopes, always perseveres" (1 Cor. 13:4–7).

When you have the gospel and the fruit of the Spirit in your heart, truth and love will come out of your mouth. "A good man brings good things out of the good stored up in his heart, and an evil man brings evil things out of the evil stored up in his heart. For the mouth speaks what the heart is full of" (Luke 6:45). It is simple replacement. If good things are in your heart, evil will not be there, and a lie cannot come out of your mouth.

To keep the fruit of the Spirit in your heart, practice immediate confession of sin. To keep the truth in your heart, apply Psalm 119:11: "I have hidden your word in my heart that I might not sin against you."

> Do your best to present yourself to God as one approved, a workman who does not need to be ashamed and who correctly handles the word of truth. (2 Tim. 2:15)

> All Scripture is God-breathed and is useful for teaching, rebuking, correcting and training in righteousness, so that the man of God may be thoroughly equipped for every good work. (2 Tim. 3:16–17)

I had a self-righteous attitude until a few weeks after I turned twenty, when I became a Christian. I reasoned that I was better than other people because I did not use foul language or slang, or drink, smoke, or have sex. I had no hesitation about lying. I lied to my mother, to all of my high school teachers, and to my older brother. I wanted people to think well of me, so I stretched the truth. (Not really—there was not even any truth in it to stretch.) I had the two primary characteristics of Satan: pride and lying.

There is no such thing as a white lie. That term claims that sin is sinless. It is a euphemism to justify lying. Lying is sin against God. If you are a Christian, you must confess the lie immediately. You may also need to confess to the people you have lied to.

There are several kinds of lying.

- Bearing false witness against your neighbor. "You shall not give false testimony against your neighbor" (Exod. 20:16).
- Lying for fun/joking. "Like a madman shooting firebrands or deadly arrows is a man who deceives his neighbor and says, 'I was only joking!'"(Prov. 26:18–19).
- Lying about your own history—bragging about things that are not true.
- Stretching the truth—exaggerating a true story to make it more exciting.
- Slander—telling lies about someone else. "But now you must rid yourselves of all such things as these: anger, rage, malice, slander, and filthy language from your lips" (Col. 3:8).

Lying is done by men, women, children, politicians, and nations. Lying is the sin that goes with all other sins. If a man is a thief, he lies about it—sin to cover sin. Lying is the native language of the enemy, and the world belongs to the enemy.

> We know that we are children of God, and that the whole world is under the control of the evil one. (1 John 5:19)

> They exchanged the truth of God for a lie, and worshiped and served created things rather than the Creator—who is forever praised. Amen. (Rom. 1:25)

> You belong to your father the devil, and you want to carry out your father's desire. He was a murderer from the beginning, not holding to the truth, for there is no truth in him. When he lies, he speaks his native language, for he is a liar and the father of lies. (John 8:44)

Those who have been saved from the enemy are not allowed to lie; it is no longer their nature. "Do not lie to each other, since you have taken off your old self with its practices and have put on the new self, which is being renewed in knowledge in the image of its Creator" (Col. 3:9–10).

How do we quit lying? Not by trying to quit. That won't work. You can only quit by having a godly sorrow and repenting of your lying. If you are not a Christian, this repentance is done by admitting that you cannot save yourself, that you are convicted of sin, and calling upon Jesus as Lord. Your lying will be forgiven along with everything else.

Revelation 22:14 describes saved people this way: "Blessed are those who wash their robes, that they may have the right to the tree of life and may go through the gates into the city." Verse 15 describes the unsaved who are not allowed to enter the city: "Outside are the dogs, those who practice magic arts, the sexually immoral, the murderers, the idolaters and everyone who loves and practices *falsehood*." Who cannot enter the city? Those who *love and practice lying*.

Ask God to show you all the lies you have not confessed. Then confess them. "If we confess our sins, he is faithful and just and will forgive us our sins and purify us from all unrighteousness" (1 John 1:9).

Recently I was asked how to keep children from lying. There are several answers to that question. The first is: you can't. They are born liars. My parents were successful in teaching me to stay away from profanity, slang, tobacco, alcohol, and girls. They were not successful in teaching me not to lie. I lied my way through high school.

The second answer is to teach them the negative consequences of lying: if caught, an immediate, hard spanking. This will thin down the lying. However, it will also help them to figure out how to not get caught.

The third is to teach them the everlasting consequences of lying.

> Nothing impure will ever enter it, nor will anyone who does what is shameful or deceitful, but only those whose names are written in the Lamb's book of life. (Rev. 21:27)

> Outside are the dogs, those who practice magic arts, the sexually immoral, the murderers, the idolaters and everyone who loves and practices falsehood. (Rev. 22:15)

When we teach this judgment, we should also teach the gospel of Jesus Christ. When people receive Christ, several things happen: They are washed, made clean, purified, and sanctified (1 Cor. 6:11); their names are written in the book of life (Rev. 21:27); and they are dead to sin (Rom. 6:1–2). As it was normal for an unbeliever to lie, so it is not normal for a believer to lie.

If you already know your child is guilty of something, do not ask him if he did it. He will say that he did not do it. You have just helped him lie. Then you have to spank him for lying on top of whatever else he did. As they say, "Ask me no questions, and I'll tell you no lies."

Instead, tell him that you know that he did it, and ask him if he would he like to tell you why. He may still lie, but it will be harder for him to come up with a story.

If the story is obviously fiction, tell him you do not want to hear any more.

How do you keep from lying? Recognize that lies are from Satan. Stay filled with the fruit of the Spirit. Recognize that your old man has been put off and lying is no longer normal.

If you have lied, confess to God. If you do not confess the lies you have already told, it is almost certain that you will lie again.

CHAPTER 13

How to Be Free from a Critical Spirit

By Bessie Wilson

*T*he first meaning of *critic* in the dictionary is "a person who forms or expresses judgments of people or things according to certain standards or values."[12] There is nothing wrong with the ability to critique in this way. We do it all the time. There are critics in art, music, education, and government. Civilization requires critical people to keep us in line; otherwise we would slump to an awful place.

12. *Webster's New World Dictionary*, 2nd college ed., (1984). s.v. "critic."

Another meaning of critic is someone who censures or finds fault. When that is done well, it is all right. You can legitimately find fault with something that is bad. The process of criticism itself is not a problem. A critical *mind* is necessary.

WRONG JUDGMENT

What is the difference between a critical *mind* and a critical *spirit?* When you have a critical spirit, the pleasure of criticism takes over, and you set yourself up as judge or sheriff. A critical spirit is a spirit that is faultfinding or censorious of other people. This faultfinding is not for the other person's good but is judgmental, condemning, and self-righteous.

Linked with criticism is the word *discernment,* which is the ability to see and compare. Years ago, when I first started Christian work, I asked God to give me the spirit of discernment. This is important for a Bible teacher. You need to be able to see error when it creeps in. God gave me the gift of discernment, but years later He convicted me deeply of the abuse of that gift.

> Why do you look at the speck of sawdust in your brother's eye and pay no attention to the plank in your own eye? How can you say to your brother, "Let me take the speck out of your eye," when all the time there is a plank in your own eye? You hypocrite, first take the plank out of your own eye, and then you will see clearly to remove the speck from your brother's eye. (Matt. 7:3–5)

Jesus said, "Why do you look at the speck of saw-dust when there is a plank in your own eye?" It's like having a splinter in the other person's eye and a tele-phone pole in your own.

We all have a blind spot somewhere. We don't know everything. However, the ability to see error starkly in someone else can sometimes make us think we do know everything. We have a very difficult time turn-ing the spotlight back on ourselves and saying, "What about you?" Even the best driver cannot see every-thing. It's impossible. When we're driving, we need to be aware of the blind spots. Spiritually speaking, Christian friendships help us to determine where our own personal blind spots are.

I did not think I had a blind spot. I was a missionary. I had been told so often that I was very spiritual that I believed it. It took marriage to bring out my blind spots. The major one was self-pity. I was very proud of my abil-ity to never be angry, to accept everything. If there was trouble of any kind, I would suffer rather than say any-thing. I honestly thought it was a great virtue. I had been told how levelheaded I was and how easy I was to get along with, and I believed it. Then Jim pointed out that if I was offended and became quiet, I was as hard to get along with as if I had blown my top. I couldn't buy that at first. I had grown up with a sister who blew her top, and I thought it was the most dreadful thing to live with. But Jim said, "Which is worse, to make the house cold for three days, or to have fifteen minutes of fireworks?"

It wasn't until Jim pointed it out to me that I remembered something my dear father said to me when I still lived at home. I had four brothers and a sister, and I was the youngest. The dish washing duty had been lodged with me. All my siblings would say they had taken their turn, and now it was mine. There I was stuck with washing the dishes for all those people.

One evening, I had my hands in the dish water, feeling very much a martyr, and my father came up behind me and said, "Bess, you know we wouldn't help you for the world. You're having such a good time."

Self-pity can be a luxury to be indulged in. You can feel like you're the world's best martyr. "Am I not stuck with all this, and am I not being patient about it?"

Marriage opened my eyes to that blind spot quickly. However, I did not have a critical spirit in my early marriage. It took having four children. As a mother, you are forced into a position of leadership in the home. The meals, the laundry, the general running of the home are all your jurisdiction. I don't know where it started, but somewhere in that first thirty years of marriage, I became the sheriff of the house. I was critical about everyone else's performance and about my own. I didn't see any good anywhere. I looked at our minister in town with a critical eye. When Jim talked to me about what was being done with CCM, I didn't say what I thought was good. I said, "Well, that is wrong, and I don't like this, and I don't like that." My good ability to judge got out of hand. I set myself up as the sole determiner of right and wrong. I criticized everything and everyone. As I sat in this position, I had a great, big plank in my own eye.

The critical spirit is based in pride. How so? When we make a critical evaluation of something, we make ourselves the final authority. We are setting ourselves above it. "I wouldn't do that. I wouldn't say that. How can this person act like that and be a Christian? Why did they do that? Why did they say that?" Before you know it, you have forgotten that you do those things, too. Why do you look at the speck in your neighbor's eye when there is a plank in your own?

A critical spirit commonly causes depression. When you have a negative view of everyone, and all you can see are the wrongs, you become very depressed. I was unable to thank God for beauty. I was unable to thank Him for the growth I saw in different individuals. Instead of rejoicing in the progress I saw with people in our Christian work and counseling, I saw only how much more they needed. I became more and more miserable. Then in May 1979, we talked of taking a sabbatical and going to Canada for a few months. I realized that I was looking forward to the sabbatical to get myself straightened out; and the Lord said to me, "I want to straighten you out right now."

I was deeply convicted of the sin of having a critical spirit. I couldn't share it with anyone. I knew if I tried, I would cry my heart out and not be able to finish, so I put it down on paper. In a letter to my husband and children, I wrote: "There have been occasions in my life when God has blessed me *in spite of* what I know is 'an iceberg of judgments' resulting in bitterness of heart. Most of my Christian life I have been in Christian leadership, and I see this sin (a critical spirit) now as a peril in leadership. Having once prayed for discernment, I see now it needs a balance. Oswald Chambers said that discernment is given not to criticize, but to intercede. I have become a 'sheriff' in the Christian community, in my home and marriage."

I wrote much more than this and received nothing but love and understanding from my family. In repentance, I cried before the Lord in agony to have this sin removed from me and to be forgiven. Never before or since have I been so repentant.

At the time, I was leading a noon Bible study on the University of Idaho campus. We were working through the book of Micah and came to this verse: "I will bear the indignation of the Lord, because I have sinned against Him, until He pleads my case and executes justice for me. He will bring me forth to the light; I will see His righteousness" (Micah 7:9 NKJV). I was overwhelmed with my sin and thinking, "This is the way I always have been, and this is the way I always will be." God used this verse to say to me, "No, I want to take it from you."

I wanted to be delivered from the critical spirit, and, thank God, He did deliver me. Does that mean I have not had the critical spirit since? Yes, I have, but I can identify it now faster and be rid of it.

RIGHT JUDGMENT

> Do not judge, or you too will be judged. For in the
> same way you judge others, you will be judged, and
> with the measure you use, it will be measured to
> you. Why do you look at the speck of sawdust in your
> brother's eye and pay no attention to the plank in
> your own eye? How can you say to your brother, "Let
> me take the speck out of your eye," when all the time
> there is a plank in your own eye? You hypocrite, first
> take the plank out of your own eye, and then you will
> see clearly to remove the speck from your brother's
> eye. (Matt. 7:1–5)

You are not a help to anyone, including yourself, if
you are filled with a critical spirit. However, Jesus did
not say to forget criticism. He said to get rid of your
own plank, and then you will be able to see clearly to
help someone else.

There are two dangers in the misuse of Jesus's statement in Matthew 7. First, we can fail to read to the end
of verse five and realize that we need to see clearly before we try to remove the speck from our brother's eye.
Sometimes the speck in the other person's eye doesn't
seem like a speck at all once your own plank is gone.

Second, we can practice the nonjudgmental attitude to the extent that we throw out discernment. This
becomes the sin of tolerance. Tolerance allows people to
avoid correcting their own behavior and that of others.

Every time I bring up the subject of judgment, some dear Christian says, "Now, now, Bessie, the Scripture says, 'Judge not, that you be not judged.'" This verse is often quoted to quell criticism, and the person using the quote goes away satisfied. Yet Jesus did not say don't judge. He said to judge with *righteous* judgment (John 7:24). Jesus told us to remove the planks from our own eyes so that we could see clearly to *help others*.

Galatians 6:1 gives us a guideline on how to handle criticism. "Brothers, if someone is caught in a sin, *you who are spiritual* should restore him gently. But watch yourself, or you also may be tempted" (Gal. 6:1). When you see something wrong in a person, in a situation, in a church, can you get past this qualification: "you who are spiritual"? You are not spiritually competent to judge until you are positive that plank is out of your own eye.

The first step when we see something wrong is to go to the Lord in prayer and say, "Father, I'm concerned about this, but before I go off carelessly, willfully, I ask You search me." Psalm 139:23–24 (NKJV) says, "Search me, O God, and know my heart; try me, and know my anxieties; and see if there is any wicked way in me, and lead me in the way everlasting." Many times, the Lord has said to me, "Bessie, you're not qualified. You can pray about this situation, but you are not eligible to fix it."

You can only go and help someone if you are spiritual. "Spiritual" does not mean pious. To be spiritual is to be in tune with God, to have God's Spirit controlling your spirit so that you don't go and do damage to other people. It means having your own sins confessed up to date and being right with God yourself.

"You who are spiritual *restore such a one in a spirit of gentleness . . .*" (Gal. 6:1 NKJV). God says to restore people gently. When you are critical, you are first of all *not* to go set people right. Isn't that our motivation so often? "Someone's got to tell these people! And I'm the one to do it." No. Even if you succeed in convincing them that they are wrong, setting them right is not the same as restoring them. Restoring means getting that person back to their spiritual walk with God. Jumping on other people's sins is like jumping on sparks to put them out. You just fan them into a flame instead. Then you wonder why other people don't respond to you.

Restore them *gently*. The KJV says, "in a spirit of meekness." You must not be overbearing. You must not be cruel. You need to be tough sometimes, but you can be tough *and* gentle. Tough love means not giving room to sin.

"Restore such a one in a spirit of gentleness, *considering yourself lest you also be tempted*" (Gal. 6:1 NKJV). Watch yourself. Often the things that bug us the most are the things that we also are capable of doing and need to be careful about. Paul says, "Therefore you are inexcusable, O man, whoever you are who judge, for in whatever you judge another you condemn yourself; for you who judge practice the same things" (Rom. 2:1 NKJV). In other words, it takes one to know one. We see this sin in someone else because we've been there. In one way, I feel spiritually capable of talking about a critical spirit precisely because I have been there. But if I still had a critical spirit, I wouldn't dare! Because I have allowed God to deal with it, I am able and want to help anyone else who has it.

Leviticus 19:15 gives another scriptural guideline for judging correctly: "Do not pervert justice; do not show partiality to the poor or favoritism to the great, but judge your neighbor fairly." Just because a person is poor does not mean that he has nobility of thought or action; a look at welfare cases might jolt you to a more realistic stance on this. The rich and famous also cannot bear the scrutiny of the Word of God. In his letter, James warns us about treatment of poor and rich in the church: "don't show favoritism" (James 2:1). Avoid generalizations. Some poor people are haughty and proud, and some rich people are humble and gracious. Don't rush into putting everybody into one judgment category.

There are many lists in the Word by which we are to judge ourselves and others. In 1 Peter 4:17, Peter says that "it is time for judgment to begin with the family of God." In 1 Corinthians 11:29, Paul points out that we can eat and drink judgment on ourselves if we do not recognize the body of the Lord as we receive communion. He went on to say that "if we judged ourselves, we would not come under judgment" (v. 31). In 1 Corinthians 6, Paul encourages us to judge disputes in the church—appointing "even men of little account" (v. 4) to do so. This was to discourage going to law before unbelievers. "Do you not know that the wicked will not inherit the kingdom of God? Do not be deceived: Neither the sexually immoral nor idolaters nor adulterers nor male prostitutes nor homosexual offenders nor thieves nor the greedy nor drunkards nor slanders nor swindlers will inherit the kingdom of God" (vv. 9–10).

We can conclude from Scripture that we are not to be judgmental about others, but we are certainly to discern our own spiritual needs and theirs in the light of Scripture and seek to help others after we have been cleansed ourselves.

Wouldn't it be better just to mind your own business and not get into any situation where you had to correct another? No. You would not be a good Christian if you did that. No one lives to himself. Love that cares reaches out and even interferes in other people's business. You just have to be careful that you are in the right condition for it.

I had a neighbor in Annapolis who said, "I just don't let people come to see me. I don't have friends, but then again, I don't have any enemies." It was true; she had nothing. She did not understand how we could stand the constant stream of people coming to our house for counseling and fellowship. Not having friends or enemies is not Christian. We are here to help each other.

Oswald Chambers said that discernment is given to us, not to criticize, but to intercede. If you see someone at fault, the first thing to do is pray for them. Say, "I will not allow myself one word until I have talked to God about this situation." It is wonderful to intercede for people. I have noticed that if I have prayed for someone, when I meet them I am looking for encouraging signs of answered prayer. I am not looking for more faults. The more good I see coming out of answered prayer, the more encouraged I am. Then I pray for an opportunity with that person, and God gives it.

So much harm is done because we do not pray. The Scripture tells us to pray one for another (James 5:16). Who knows what that person is suffering? At Christmas one year, Jim was very concerned for a family in town, and he was in his study praying for them. He heard me call, "Jim, so-and-so is walking up to the door." It was the very person he was praying for. They had a long and very helpful visit. He had great joy in talking to them because he had already talked to God about it.

Every time you see a need in someone else, let it guide you to prayer. Then if the Lord should tap you on the shoulder and say, "I think you are ready now to go," say, "Thank you, Lord. I will go, and I will go in the spirit of meekness, knowing that I too could be tempted."

Since that time the Lord dealt with me, I believe He has made me gentler with people than I ever was before.

May I remind you again of Galatians 6:1: "Brothers, if someone is caught in a sin, you who are spiritual should restore him gently. But watch yourself, or you also may be tempted."

"Finally, brothers, whatever is true, whatever is noble, whatever is right, whatever is pure, whatever is lovely, whatever is admirable—if anything is excellent or praiseworthy—think about such things" (Phil. 4:8).

CHAPTER 14

How to Be Free from Complaining

Do everything without complaining or arguing, so that you may become blameless and pure, children of God without fault in a crooked and depraved generation, in which you shine like stars in the universe as you hold out the word of life, in order that I may boast in the day of Christ that I did not labor for nothing. But even if I am poured out like a drink offering on the sacrifice and service coming from your faith, I am glad and rejoice with all of you. So you too should be glad and rejoice with me. (Phil. 2:14–18)

*P*hilippians tells us how to be blameless and pure, not when we get to heaven, but *now* in the midst of all the wickedness around us: do everything without complaining or arguing.

Unlike some of the other sins discussed in this book (anger, lying, stealing), you may not realize just how sinful complaining is.

What does God think of complaining?

> Now when the people complained, it displeased the LORD; for the LORD heard it, and His anger was aroused. So the fire of the LORD burned among them, and consumed some in the outskirts of the camp. (Num. 11:1 NKJV)

> All the Israelites grumbled against Moses and Aaron, and the whole assembly said to them, "If only we had died in Egypt! Or in this desert! Why is the LORD bringing us to this land only to let us fall by the sword? Our wives and children will be taken as plunder. Wouldn't it be better for us to go back to Egypt?" . . . .

> The LORD said to Moses and Aaron: "How long will this wicked community grumble against me? I have heard the complaints of these grumbling Israelites. So tell them, 'As surely as I live, declares the LORD, I will do to you the very thing I heard you say: In this wilderness your bodies will fall—every one of you twenty years old or more who was counted in the census and who has grumbled against me. Not one of you will enter the land I swore with uplifted hand

to make your home, except Caleb son of Jephunneh
and Joshua son of Nun.'" (Num. 14:2–3, 26–30)

Then they despised the pleasant land;
They did not believe His word,
But complained in their tents,
And did not heed the voice of the LORD.
Therefore He raised His hand in an oath against
    them,
To overthrow them in the wilderness,
To overthrow their descendants among the nations,
And to scatter them in the lands.
(Psalm 106:24–27 NKJV)

Nor let us commit sexual immorality, as some of them
did, and in one day twenty-three thousand fell . . . nor
complain, as some of them also complained, and
were destroyed by the destroyer. Now all these things
happened to them as examples, and they were written for our admonition, upon whom the ends of the
ages have come. (1 Cor. 10:8, 10–11 NKJV)

Make a study of complaining in the Scriptures,
and you will find that it does not turn out well for the
complainers.

For the wrath of God is revealed from heaven against
all ungodliness and unrighteousness of men, who
suppress the truth in unrighteousness . . . because,
although they knew God, they did not glorify Him as
God, nor were thankful, but became futile in their

thoughts, and their foolish hearts were darkened.
(Rom. 1:18, 21 NKJV)

Do not grumble against one another, brethren, lest
you be condemned. Behold, the Judge is standing at
the door! (James 5:9 NKJV)

Have you ever known a chronic complainer? Does
it bother you to hear someone complain, complain,
complain?

Have *you* ever complained?

Generally speaking, complaining is limited to
the person who doesn't get to make the decisions.
Consequently, men complain about what happens at
work, and women complain about their husbands. The
person who always gets the free choice doesn't complain, unless he complains against God. Women have a
bigger temptation to complain, because they are (like it
or not) on the dirty end of the stick.

Our democratic society considers fairness to be almost the highest virtue there is. Because things are not
fair, we complain. Things *aren't* fair. That is true. How
do we fix that? The trouble is that Scripture does not
tell us to do everything fairly. It tells us to knock off the
complaining. Well, we could knock off complaining if
things would just be fair, right?

Although fairness is a high virtue in an egalitarian
society, it is *not* a high virtue in the Bible. Mercy is a virtue. Justice is a virtue. Righteousness is a virtue. Aren't
they the same thing? No. Fairness says everything must

be equal. Righteousness and justice may not be equal. God is just, God is righteous, God is merciful, God is loving, God is kind. God is *not* fair. People complain about Him for that. He's not fair. True! But who said He's supposed to be?

We cannot complain against justice, or righteousness, or mercy, or holiness, or love, or kindness. There is no basis for that. Instead, we have picked an arbitrary standard called fairness, and we complain against it.

Many people believe that the Word of God is inspired. It is amazing how we will fight hard for the inspiration of Scripture—until we read it. Until we have to *do* it. Then we've got "reasons" to disobey. Or reinterpret.

Jesus said, "For the kingdom of heaven is like a landowner who went out early in the morning to hire workers for his vineyard. He agreed to pay them a denarius for the day and sent them into his vineyard" (Matt. 20:1–2). He agreed with them to pay them a denarius a day. That's what *they* asked for, and he agreed.

"About the third hour he went out and saw others standing in the marketplace doing nothing. He told them, 'You also go and work in my vineyard, and I will pay you whatever is right.' So they went" (vv. 3–5). Notice that he said he would pay them, not whatever was *fair*, but "whatever was *right*."

He went out again about the sixth hour and the ninth hour and did the same thing. About the eleventh hour he went out and found still others standing around. He asked them, "Why have you been standing here all day long doing nothing?"

"Because no one has hired us," they answered.

He said to them, "You also go and work in my vineyard."

When evening came, the owner of the vineyard said to his foreman, "Call the workers and pay them their wages, beginning with the last ones hired and going on to the first."

The workers who were hired about the eleventh hour came and each received a denarius. So when those came who were hired first, they expected to receive more. But each one of them also received a denarius. When they received it, they began to grumble against the landowner. (vv. 6–11)

One thing you will notice about complainers is that very seldom do they complain to the boss. They complain among themselves and within the gossip circle. I was in the Navy for nine years on several different ships. For some time, I was on a destroyer called the *USS Brush*. It was nicknamed the *Be-No Brush*. What did that mean? There'd be no liberty, there'd be no cake, there'd be no movie, there'd be no . . . They were complainers. The whole ship complained.

"They began to grumble against the landowner. 'These men who were hired last worked only one hour,' they said, 'and you have made them equal to us who have

borne the burden of the work and the heat of the day'"
(vv. 11–12). This is a request for him to be egalitarian.

Before we get to the landowner's answer, let me ask
you a question. Would you have grumbled if you were
in this position? You probably would have.

"But he answered one of them, 'Friend, I am not being unfair to you. Didn't you agree to work for a denarius?" (v. 13). You agreed to work for that amount. What's
your complaint? You've been happy all day thinking
you're going to get a denarius, and you earned it. Now
you're unhappy. You want something you didn't earn
because you think someone else got something he
didn't earn.

"Take your pay and go. I want to give the man who
was hired last the same as I gave you. Don't I have the
right to do what I want with my own money?" (vv. 14–
15a). True or false? He does.

"Or are you envious because I am generous?" (v.
15b). Yes.

Is generosity a sin? No.

Is envy a sin? You know the answer.

The inequality in this story was not based upon the
landowner *taking* anything away from anyone. The inequality was that he gave more to someone else. "So
the last will be first, and the first will be last" (v. 16).
Although I have made the application to complaining,
Jesus's teaching here was on salvation. He was saying
that people who have lived for Christ since they were
four are no different than people who receive Christ

when they are ninety. They are both saved by grace. They are both saved by the generosity, the mercy, and the righteousness of God. "Do you mean to say I can live like the devil all my life and at the last receive Jesus Christ?" Yes. However, you don't know when the last is going to be. When people do receive Jesus Christ on the last day, they will regret not having done it on the first day. The person who lives for Jesus Christ all his life is not a loser.

Jesus is saying that grace isn't fair. Grace is righteousness and godliness, but not fairness. If we got *fairness*, none of us would go to glory. If we got what we fairly deserved, we would all go to hell. *Thank God He's not fair!*

I grew up with the fairness doctrine, not with the gospel. I did not become a Christian until I was twenty. That's a hard time to shake your assumptions about life. Fairness is good (or so I thought), and Christian things are good, and I wound up equating the two. When I was rearing my children, and it came to serving them peaches at the end of dinner, I would take four children's dishes, and I would put one slice of peach in each dish. Then I would start over again putting a second slice in each one, and so on, so that it came out equal. Why did I do that? I was afraid that if I put too many peaches in one dish, the other children would say, "Dad, that's not fair!"

There is a story told about Abraham Lincoln. He was walking along the street with two of his boys, and they were squabbling. One of his friends said, "Abe, what's wrong with your boys?" He said, "The same thing that's wrong with the rest of the world. I've got three chestnuts, and each one of them wants two." People don't mind unfairness if it's unfair in their favor. They only object to unfairness if they are on the short end.

I learned a lot from my children as I watched them raise their own kids. In my view, they did a better job with their children than we did with them. Here is one of the ways they did it. Doug, my oldest son, told me one time that when he served ice cream, sometimes he would give one of the three kids a great, heaping bowlful and the other two a normal helping. He did not allow them to say, "That's not fair." The person who says, "That's not fair!" is the boss. If we submit to that, any complainer gets to dictate—to God, to his parents, or to anyone else. Doug's kids knew their father was not fair, and he didn't have to be fair. "Fair" was a dirty word in their house, and it was not used. Your father is generous, kind, and gracious, and don't count on yourself getting the big dish next time. You might, or you might not. Doug didn't always do that, but having done it a few times, he effectively removed fairness as a means to complaining.[13] Even though I tried to treat our children fairly, I still didn't allow complaining. It was

13. If someone really was consistently treating one child with a great favoritism over the others, that is not a question of being unfair. (It may be unfair, but that is not the real problem.) That is unrighteousness. God says He is not a respecter of persons. He doesn't play favorites, so we should not play favorites, either. It is unjust.

wonderful to see my children treating their kids, in effect, unfairly, and they still didn't get to complain.

Complaining looks wrong when we see it in other people, but when we see it in ourselves, it's "justified." We can legitimately complain because we've been mistreated . . . right?

> If someone strikes you on the right cheek, turn to him the other also. And if someone wants to sue you and take your tunic, let him have your cloak as well. If someone forces you to go one mile, go with him two miles . . . . Love your enemies and pray for those who persecute you, that you may be sons of your Father in heaven. (Matt. 5:39–41, 44–45)

> If your enemy is hungry, give him food to eat; if he is thirsty, give him water to drink. (Prov. 25:21 NKJV)

Perhaps people are lying about you, stealing from you, or gossiping about you on Facebook. Maybe it is much, much worse than that. Either way, you have been sinned against. Perhaps you aren't a complainer, but what has happened to you is *wrong!* In this situation, complaining is justified.

Wrong. That is the world's answer to your situation. The apostle Paul said to do everything without complaining. In Colossians, he says, "Whatever you do, do it heartily, as to the Lord and not to men, knowing that from the Lord you will receive the reward of the

inheritance; for you serve the Lord Christ" (Col. 3:23–24
NKJV). If I am doing something heartily as to the Lord,
how can I complain? I can't. According to the Bible, I
am to do *everything* without complaining, and do everything heartily unto the Lord. Whatever I do, I do in
the name of the Lord Jesus. Can I complain in the name
of the Lord Jesus? If something is truly unjust, perhaps.
But if your sense of justice is based upon fairness, it is
probably a wrong sense.

We have merged humanism with Christianity. Our
culture has become more authoritative in our eyes than
the Bible is. It shouldn't be. I don't mean the world's
culture; I mean the *evangelical* culture. If we went according to the Scripture and the Bible's standards, we
would wind up crossing the mainstream Christian culture very much. When you became a Christian, you
found out that you were not at home in the world anymore and that the world would be critical of you. You
knew that you had to be willing to die to the opinions
of the world and not care what the world thought. But
then perhaps there came a time when you decided to
follow the Lord all the way with your whole heart, and
you found that you were out of step with the church.
People thought you were super-righteous or pious or
that you thought you were better than others.

Several decades ago, I got to know a student at the
University of Idaho who was not a Christian. We became friends, so he felt free to talk to me. One day, he
was in the bookstore in Moscow, and he confided in

me that he knew what was wrong with the Christians in town.

"What's wrong?" I asked.

"They're all self-righteous," he said. "They've got a holier-than-thou attitude; they look down on other people."

"Oh?" I said. "I don't know anybody like that."

"I know lots."

"Name one!"

He named one. It was another student at UI, one I knew well. "He doesn't have a holier-than-thou attitude. He's doing his best just to keep his own head above water. He doesn't have time to look down on anyone else."

He believed me. "OK, then why do I *think* he's got a holier-than-thou attitude?"

"Oh," I said, "he *is* holier than thou."

In every church, there are people who want to be on the periphery of holiness because it's easier to complain there, where the pastor doesn't hear it.

Complaining is an ungrateful, unthankful, unhappy exercise. We are to rejoice in the Lord always. If I am complaining, I am not rejoicing in the Lord. Suppose someone is unrighteous, unjust, unkind, and does all kinds of bad things to you. The Bible says *that* is when you are to rejoice. It doesn't say that's when you get to complain!

"But it wasn't just unfair—it was wrong!" Ah! Then rejoice in the Lord. Read 1 Peter. Read the Sermon on the Mount. That is when we are to be thankful. That is when we are to be praising God. That is not when we are to be ungrateful. If I complain, I have just lost my joy in the Lord, not because of the other person's sin, but because of *my* complaining.

How do you get out of the habit of complaining? This is the solution: "And be ye thankful" (Col. 3:15b KJV). Confess the complaining as sin and start thanking God. "Give thanks in all circumstances; for this is God's will for you in Christ Jesus" (1 Thess. 5:18). It is impossible to complain while you are busy thanking God.

Is the climate of your workplace complaining and arguing? Is it saturated with that? You certainly don't have to participate in it.

"Doesn't God care about the trouble I'm in?" Yes, He does. We are not called to be stoics, pretending that nothing can touch us. If you have a real problem, don't complain about it, but do take it to the Lord.

If you find yourself complaining, call it sin. Confess it and get back in the joy of the Lord. There is no sense in you stumbling because someone else is in sin.

CHAPTER 15

How to Be Free from Peer Pressure

P eer pressure is a basic tool of the devil. It crops up in every society and school in the world. There are two evils to peer pressure: 1) paying attention to and caving in to the pressure and 2) being part of the group that gives the pressure.

Copying people who insist on your copying them is not the same as voluntary imitation. Imitation is following someone you respect with no pressure from the one you are imitating. It is normally for your good.

Peer pressure is forcing conformity to a moral standard that is increasingly lower. Because we are not created by God to be loners, we have an instinct to belong to a body of people. The basic body is the family: a father, a mother, grandparents, brothers, sisters, aunts, uncles, and cousins. We are born into a family. It is a good thing. We are meant to be nursed, loved, played with, provided for, and other expressions that make us very secure. We grow up, get married, and have another family that is secure.

The enemy wants to destroy this place of love and security. He does it by isolating each member from the rest of the family and getting that member to conform to lower standards than the family's standard. This includes the cliques at school: popular kids, brainy kids, jocks, and the kids who do not fit into any of the other groups. They make their own rules.

Outside the family, teenage groups pressure kids into drugs, drinking, sex, and stealing. Within the family, to break it up, the enemy will encourage verbal, physical, and/or sexual abuse of the wife and the kids. There are clubs of all kinds, such as fraternities and sororities. Because we want to belong, we voluntarily submit to the fraternity's rules. All of these are peer pressures to a different standard.

What do we do about this? There is another family that will keep us healthy; it is the body of Christ. You also get into this family by being born into it.

> In reply Jesus declared, "I tell you the truth, no one can see the kingdom of God unless he is born again." (John 3:3)

Now the body is not made up of one part but of
many. (1 Cor. 12:14)

There are many members in this body. Members receive characteristics that are unique to the body. These
come with the membership. Here is a list of them: "But
the fruit of the Spirit is love, joy, peace, patience, kindness, goodness, faithfulness, gentleness and self-control. Against such things there is no law. Those who
belong to Christ Jesus have crucified the sinful nature
with its passions and desires. Since we live by the Spirit,
let us keep in step with the Spirit" (Gal. 5:22–25).

And the members have other benefits:

- They love each other.
- They love their enemies.
- They love their wives and children.
- They love God.
- They love their neighbors.

This love is not friendship, nor is it sexual; it is sacrificial love for the other person's good.

This body is the body of Christ of which He is the
head. When we are members of the body of Christ, we
become much better members of our family.

If you are a member of other bodies (gangs, fraternities, etc.), they will see the difference in you, and they
will not like it. They will try to get you to be immoral
again. If that fails, you will be ostracized.

Be imitators of God, therefore, as dearly loved children and live a life of love, just as Christ loved us and gave himself up for us as a fragrant offering and sacrifice to God.

But among you there must not be even a hint of sexual immorality, or of any kind of impurity, or of greed, because these are improper for God's holy people. Nor should there be obscenity, foolish talk or coarse joking, which are out of place, but rather thanksgiving. For of this you can be sure: No immoral, impure or greedy person—such a man is an idolater—has any inheritance in the kingdom of Christ and of God. Let no one deceive you with empty words, for because of such things God's wrath comes on those who are disobedient. Therefore do not be partners with them.

For you were once darkness, but now you are light in the Lord. Live as children of light (for the fruit of the light consists in all goodness, righteousness and truth) and find out what pleases the Lord. Have nothing to do with the fruitless deeds of darkness, but rather expose them. For it is shameful even to mention what the disobedient do in secret. But everything exposed by the light becomes visible . . . . (Eph. 5:1–13)

The Apostle Paul describes your new life as light. All things become visible when they are exposed by the light. People do not want their deeds exposed. They will try to get you back in the darkness because they cannot stand the light.

> Yet to all who received him, to those who believed in his name, he gave the right to become children of God. (John 1:12)

> Come to me, all you who are weary and burdened, and I will give you rest. Take my yoke upon you and learn from me, for I am gentle and humble in heart, and you will find rest for your souls. (Matt. 11:28–29)

Become a member of the body of Christ, and your life will be immeasurably different. You will still encounter peer pressure, but you will be able to stand against it.

If you are already a Christian and are guilty of being pressured by the world, there is something wrong.

- You have not confessed sins in your life.
- You have not been reading the Bible.
- You have not been praying.
- You are not in regular fellowship with other members of the body of Christ.

If you are a Christian and walking in the light, you might not be a leader, but you will not be a follower; you will not give in to peer pressure. Out in the world, you will not be absolutely alone. There are other members of the body of Christ out there, and you have the promises of Christ. "And surely I am with you always, to the very end of the age" (Matt. 28:20b).

One of the most common areas of conformity is profanity. Here are two excuses I have heard for foul speech. "I worked on an Alaskan fishing boat." "I work in the roundhouse of the Burlington Northern Railroad." Christians seem to think that I should understand why they speak that way.

Listen, I am ninety-two years old. When I was sixteen and seventeen, I worked in the stock yards of Omaha, Nebraska. That was followed by one year as a sailor, four years as a midshipman at the Naval Academy, and six and a half years as an officer in the U.S. Navy, most of which time I was at sea. I know the language! I do not think I ever used any of the words. Profanity is *not* necessary to communicate meaning. People use the words because other people use them. They do not use them to make sense; they use them because they are unsaved. Their hearts are dirty, so their mouths are dirty.

Seventy years ago at the Naval Academy, I walked into a classmate's room on a Sunday morning. He met me with a blast of dirty words. I reached into my pocket, pulled out a Christian tract, threw it on his desk, and said, "That will teach you to talk like that." Then I sat down on his bunk to read the Sunday comics page. A minute later, I heard someone crying. I looked up. My classmate was weeping. He said, "I did not grow up talking like that."

Remember that you are a member of the body of Christ, and don't give in to negative peer pressure. "For you were once darkness, but now you are light in the Lord. Live as children of light (for the fruit of the light consists in all goodness, righteousness and truth) and find out what pleases the Lord" (Eph. 5:8–10). If it seems like you are alone in standing against the pressure, remember that God has said, "Never will I leave you; never will I forsake you" (Heb. 13:5b).

CHAPTER 16

How to Be Free from Profanity

Many years ago, I was at a farm sale when a four-year-old boy walked by, kicked the tire of a piece of farm equipment, and said, "What's this #$&*?"

It is easy to fall into the habit of talking dirty, especially if you grew up with parents who talk that way. You pick it up the same way you learned English. You can also pick up profanity by rebellion; you say these words because you are not allowed to say them. A third way to pick it up is wanting to be accepted. You conform to the habits of the people around you, at work, at school, wherever. You may even take the lead in talking this way in order to get approval from others. It is peer pressure that people are eager to participate in. They want to join in the "fun" of the dirty vocabulary.

Profanity pervades every aspect of society, from kids in elementary school to educated men on Wall Street. It is in the universities and in the home. It is used by atheists and by housewives. It is easy to get into. It is easier to get out of, but you can't do it by trying to quit swearing.

Before I tell you how simple and easy it is to quit, let's look at what the Bible has to say about swearing. "You shall not misuse the name of the LORD your God, for the LORD will not hold anyone guiltless who misuses his name" (Exod. 20:7). God will not hold him guiltless who uses His name in vain. People who use the name God and Jesus Christ tell me that they are not using the name in vain because they did not mean anything by it. That is what "in vain" means. In vain = for nothing. *In vain* does not mean maliciously. It means thoughtlessly or in an empty or common way. People think they are not using God's name in vain because they did not "mean it." Not meaning it *is* using His name in vain; that is exactly what the term "in vain" refers to.

God will not hold you guiltless for this. He will hold you guilty for "not meaning it." Your non-motive makes you guilty. "But I tell you that men will have to give account on the day of judgment for every careless word they have spoken" (Matt. 12:36).[14]

---

14. Do I have to walk around in fear, unable to function because of this teaching about careless words? No, there is a preventative: "and we take captive every thought to make it obedient to Christ" (2 Cor. 10:5b).

There is a second type of profanity that is very common.

> Do not let any unwholesome talk come out of your mouths, but only what is helpful for building others up according to their needs, that it may benefit those who listen. (Eph. 4:29)

> Be imitators of God, therefore, as dearly loved children and live a life of love, just as Christ loved us and gave himself up for us as a fragrant offering and sacrifice to God. But among you there must not be even a hint of sexual immorality, or of any kind of impurity, or of greed, because these are improper for God's holy people. Nor should there be obscenity, foolish talk or coarse joking, which are out of place, but rather thanksgiving. (Eph. 5:1–4)

Our speech is meant to encourage others and be seasoned with thanksgiving. It should not contain unwholesome talk, obscenity, foolish talk or coarse joking. The Bible does not define these terms. The apostle Paul assumes that the people he is writing to know what he is talking about. Similarly, the English words that are commonly understood to be obscene or filthy are understood by constant usage.

Here we have a command which we are required to obey, but with no written definitions. We know the definitions. People have used obscene language for centuries, not because they did not know that it was filthy, but because they *did* know it was filthy. There is a certain delight in the use of vulgar words.

However, some people like to quibble about definitions, assuring us that the words they use are not obscene; their definition is different, or the words are just colorful, or poetic, or it is the hearer who has the problem or the dirty mind.

"The good man brings good things out of the good stored up in his heart, and the evil man brings evil things out of the evil stored up in his heart. For out of the overflow of his heart his mouth speaks" (Luke 6:45). Whether deliberate or thoughtless, words from the mouth come from the heart. "And He was saying, 'That which proceeds out of the man, that is what defiles the man'" (Mark 7:20 NASB).

Some people would never consider saying something dirty. Instead, they use euphemisms for dirty words. They think that they can be innocent and expressive at the same time. Examples of these euphemisms are *shucks, heck, shoot, frick,* and *dang it.* There are others that I do not have the freedom to write.

Innocent? Perhaps. Perhaps not! Jesus made a very strong statement concerning the words we use: "But I tell you that men will have to give account on the day of judgment for every careless word they have spoken. For by your words you will be acquitted and by your words you will be condemned" (Matt. 12:36–37).

Christians use synonyms to keep from taking the Lord's name in vain. Instead of *God* or *Jesus,* they will say *doggonit, gosh,* or *dag nab it.* Using a synonym is the same as using the name. Changing the sound of the word does not change the meaning. Our English name Jesus Christ was originally *Yeshua Messiah.* It is the same name.

Why is it necessary to say anything? If necessary, why must it be a substitute for God? I remember riding in a taxicab in Tokyo sixty-six years ago. The driver could not speak English, but he could say *Jesus Christ,* which he said often and with emphasis. He had learned it from American servicemen.

"The Law came in so that the transgression would increase; but where sin increased, grace abounded all the more" (Rom. 5:20 NASB). The only reason people use the Lord's name is because it is forbidden. If it were not forbidden, they would not use it. It is also a violation of Matthew 22:37–38 (NASB): "And He said to him, "'You shall love the Lord your God with all your heart, and with all your soul, and with all your mind.' This is the great and foremost commandment.'"

Look at Ephesians 5 again. "But immorality or any impurity or greed must not even be named among you, as is proper among saints; and there must be no filthiness and silly talk, or coarse jesting, which are not fitting, but rather giving of thanks. For this you know with certainty, that no immoral or impure person or covetous man, who is an idolater, has an inheritance in the kingdom of Christ and God" (vv. 5:3–5 NASB). People tell me, "These are just words; there is nothing dirty about words." If that were true, you would not use them. You use these words *because* they are dirty. You use the synonyms *because* they are dirty, too.

Some people use profanity because the people they spend time with do that. One Christian told me he talked that way because he worked in a railroad roundhouse, as if the roundhouse talk was a second language he was required to learn. They give me the same excuse for working on a salmon-fishing boat and for being in the military. I worked in the stock yards in Omaha for two years during high school. That place was an incubator for foul language. I was not a Christian; I did not speak the language, but it was there. Then I spent a year as a sailor and four years as a midshipman. I expected the dirty talk as a sailor. I did not expect it at the Naval Academy. It was there. I thought the four-letter words would disappear when I became an officer. I was wrong. I spent six and a half years as a naval officer and heard them frequently. Later I found that the president of the United States used them.

In 1969, I was running a bookstore at a Christian junior college. I printed the Ephesians 5 quote (no obscenity, foolish talk, or coarse joking) on a large poster and put it on the wall on a stairwell landing. All the students had to read it, because they had to come down that staircase in order to get their mail. One student told me that she would not use the Lord's name in vain, but she had not known that dirty talk was a sin. I do not think I believed her.

Now for the solution. "Do you not know that the wicked will not inherit the kingdom of God? Do not be deceived: Neither the sexually immoral nor idolaters nor adulterers nor male prostitutes nor homosexual offenders nor thieves nor the greedy nor drunkards nor slanderers nor swindlers will inherit the kingdom of God. And that is what some of you were. But you were washed, you were sanctified, you were justified in the name of the Lord Jesus Christ and by the Spirit of our God" (1 Cor. 6:9–11). When a man receives Christ, he receives a clean heart. Good things come out of clean hearts.

Many years ago, I was asked to teach an adult Sunday school class in another church. In this church was a man named George. He would bring his four-year-old boy to Sunday school and go across the street to Read's drugstore to drink coffee until the Sunday school class was over and he could take his boy home. One day, one of George's friends asked him, "George, why do you spend twenty-five cents for a cup of coffee when you can drink free coffee in the adult class?" That made sense to George, so he joined the class the week I was teaching.

Three weeks later, he called me. "You don't know me, but I heard you teach three weeks ago. That evening when I was putting my son to bed, I decided to pray for him. Something happened to me."

"What do you mean?" I asked.

"I have gone to the same bar five days a week for the last thirteen years. Now I am only going once a week, and I am ordering Coca-Cola. I don't know why. I love beer."

I said, "Anything else?"

"Yes. I've had a very dirty mouth for years. Now when I go to work I can't stand hearing all the profanity from my coworkers. If I say a dirty word myself, I want to bite my tongue off."

"It sounds like you have become a Christian. Come down and see me."

When he arrived, it was lunch time, so we went across the street to the Anne Arundel Coffee Shop. The owner knew both of us. When he saw us come in together, he could not believe it. He came and sat in the booth with us for a while. Finally, he said, "George, I've listened to you for thirty minutes, and you haven't said one dirty word."

The first visible evidence of a new Christian is his speech. If he has a clean heart, he has a clean mouth.

If your mouth didn't clean up when you received Christ, it is very likely that you did not receive Christ. Christ gives a clean heart, and the cleanness comes out of the mouth. If you are a Christian, then you are deliberately saying what the unbeliever says naturally. "But now you must rid yourselves of all such things as these: anger, rage, malice, slander, and filthy language from your lips" (Col. 3:8). People try all kinds of ways to quit swearing. They do not work. A *clean heart* makes it effortless. It just happens. Take some time to *confess the sins you have been letting slide*. After that, ask God to show you if there is anything you are missing. Listen, and confess what He shows you. Let Him scrub your heart clean. Once you are clean on the inside, the clean mouth will follow.

CHAPTER 17

How to Be Free from Sexual Sin

W hat is sexual sin?

- *Adultery:* "You shall not commit adultery" (Exod. 20:14).

- *Incest:* "No one is to approach any close relative to have sexual relations. I am the LORD. Do not dishonor your father by having sexual relations with your mother. She is your mother; do not have relations with her. Do not have sexual relations with your father's wife; that would dishonor your father. Do not have sexual relations with your sister, either your father's daughter or your mother's daughter, whether she was born in the same home or elsewhere. Do not have sexual relations with your son's daughter or your daughter's daughter; that would dishonor you. Do not have sexual relations with the daughter of your father's wife, born to your father; she is your sister. Do not have sexual relations with your father's sister; she is your father's close relative. Do not have sexual relations with your mother's sister, because she is your mother's close relative. Do not dishonor your father's brother by approaching his wife to have sexual relations; she is your aunt. Do not have sexual relations with your daughter-in-law. She is your son's wife; do not have relations with her. Do not have sexual relations with your brother's wife; that would dishonor your brother. Do not have sexual relations with both a woman and her daughter. Do not have sexual relations with either her son's daughter or her daughter's daughter; they are her close relatives. That is wickedness. Do not take your wife's sister as a rival wife and have sexual relations with her while your wife is living. Do not approach a woman to have sexual relations during the uncleanness of her monthly period" (Lev. 18:6–19).

- *Homosexuality:* "Do not lie with a man as one lies with a woman; that is detestable" (Lev. 18:22). "Because of this, God gave them over to shameful lusts. Even their women exchanged natural sexual relations for unnatural ones. In the same way the men also abandoned natural relations with women and were inflamed with lust for one another. Men committed shameful acts with other men, and received in themselves the due penalty for their perversion" (Rom. 1:26–27).

- *Fornication:* "It is God's will that you should be sanctified: that you should avoid sexual immorality" (1 Thess. 4:3).
- *Pornography and Voyeurism:* "But I tell you that anyone who looks at a woman lustfully has already committed adultery with her in his heart" (Matt. 5:28).
- *Bestiality:* "Do not have sexual relations with an animal and defile yourself with it. A woman must not present herself to an animal to have sexual relations with it; that is a perversion" (Lev. 18:23).

Here is what the Bible has to say about why certain people are under everlasting judgement. Pay attention.

The acts of the flesh are obvious: *sexual immorality, impurity and debauchery;* idolatry and witchcraft; hatred, discord, jealousy, fits of rage, selfish ambition, dissensions, factions and envy; drunkenness, orgies, and the like. I warn you, as I did before, that those who live like this will not inherit the kingdom of God. (Gal. 5:19–21)

Do you not know that the wicked will not inherit the kingdom of God? Do not be deceived: Neither the sexually immoral nor idolaters nor adulterers nor male prostitutes nor homosexual offenders nor thieves nor the greedy nor drunkards nor slanderers nor swindlers will inherit the kingdom of God. (1 Cor. 6:9–10)

But among you there must not be even a hint of sexual immorality, or of any kind of impurity, or of greed, because these are improper for God's holy people . . . For of this you can be sure: No immoral, impure or greedy person—such a man is an idolater—has any inheritance in the kingdom of Christ and of God. Let no one deceive you with empty words, for because of such things God's wrath comes on those who are disobedient. (Eph. 5:3, 5–6)

"Do you not know that your body is a temple of the Holy Spirit, who is in you, whom you have received from God? You are not your own; you were bought at a price. Therefore honor God with your body" (1 Cor. 6:19–20). You have risen with Christ, and you are dead to sin. Since this is true, you can make this decision: "Put to death, therefore, whatever belongs to your earthly nature: *sexual immorality, impurity, lust,* evil desires and greed, which is idolatry. Because of these, the wrath of God is coming" (Col. 3:5–6).

The first four works of the flesh in Galatians 5 are sexual sins: "adultery, fornication, uncleanness, lewdness . . . those who practice such things will not inherit the kingdom of God" (vv. 19, 21 NKJV). Four of the first five sins in 1 Corinthians 6 are sexual: "Neither fornicators, nor idolaters, nor adulterers, nor homosexuals, nor sodomites . . . will inherit the kingdom of God" (vv. 9–10 NKJV). In Ephesians 5, two out of the three sins mentioned are sexual: "fornication and all uncleanness," and "no fornicator [or] unclean person . . . has any inheritance in the kingdom of Christ and God" (vv. 3, 5 NKJV).

The wrath of God is coming on the sons of disobedience because of their sexual sin. As Christians, we are told to put to death all fornication and sexual uncleanness. These sins are what keep non-Christians out of the kingdom. Christians can commit them intentionally, while non-Christians commit them normally. Christians are tempted. Non-Christians are slaves. I understand from Christians who look at pornography that the temptation is intense. It seems impossible to them to resist or to run away from it. It is not impossible.

Remember this: these same sins are the cause of unbelievers not inheriting the kingdom of God. You are wanting to live like an unbeliever and still go to heaven. When God says to put them to death, He does not mean a slow torturous death. He means *right now*. You can do this because you have died to sin, to the law, to the basic principle of the universe.

> And that is what some of you were. But you were washed, you were sanctified, you were justified in the name of the Lord Jesus Christ and by the Spirit of our God. (1 Cor. 6:11)

> But the fruit of the Spirit is love, joy, peace, patience, kindness, goodness, faithfulness, gentleness and self-control. Against such things there is no law. *Those who belong to Christ Jesus have crucified the sinful nature with its passions and desires.* (Gal. 5:22–24)

We are new people. We are set free from the enemy. When you fall and are back looking at pictures of women, you confess your sin after the fact. You think that it is a virtue that you confess your sin. You get to sin again because you are going to confess it again. If you are doing this, you are not saturated with the Word, and you do not hate your sin. You love it.

> What shall we say, then? Shall we go on sinning so that grace may increase? By no means! We died to sin; how can we live in it any longer? (Rom. 6:1–2)

> Therefore do not let sin reign in your mortal body so that you obey its evil desires. Do not offer the parts of your body to sin, as instruments of wickedness, but rather offer yourselves to God, as those who have

been brought from death to life; and offer the parts of your body to him as instruments of righteousness. For sin shall not be your master, because you are not under law, but under grace. (Rom. 6:12–14)

Jesus prayed, "My prayer is not that you take them out of the world but that you protect them from the evil one" (John 17:15). Jesus also taught us to pray, "And lead us not into temptation, but deliver us from the evil one" (Matt. 6:13).

You are commanded to *avoid* sin, not just to confess it and sin again.

Have nothing to do with the fruitless deeds of darkness, but rather expose them. For it is shameful even to mention what the disobedient do in secret. But everything exposed by the light becomes visible . . . . (Eph. 5:11–13)

For you were once darkness, but now you are light in the Lord. Live as children of light. (Eph. 5:8)

Flee the evil desires of youth, and pursue righteousness, faith, love and peace, along with those who call on the Lord out of a pure heart. (2 Tim. 2:22)

Joseph is a good example of fleeing sin. "One day he went into the house to attend to his duties, and none of the household servants was inside. She caught him by his cloak and said, 'Come to bed with me!' But he left his cloak in her hand and ran out of the house" (Gen. 39:11–12).

Another example comes from the Apostle Paul. "Not that I have already obtained all this, or have already been made perfect, but I press on to take hold of that for which Christ Jesus took hold of me. Brothers, I do not consider myself yet to have taken hold of it. But one thing I do: Forgetting what is behind and straining toward what is ahead, I press on toward the goal to win the prize for which God has called me heavenward in Christ Jesus" (Phil. 3:12–14).

Be in the Word and in prayer daily. Stay away from all obvious places where women can be picked up, such as bars and streets where prostitutes hang out. Stay away from the kind of magazines that will cause you to get sexually aroused. Stay away from books, movies, and internet sites where sexual actions are explicit. This avoidance is simple enough.

It is not simple when a person *wants* to be tempted. You don't want to sin; you just want to be tempted. You will end up sinning.

The other half of the victory over this sin is pursuing righteousness, desiring to be like Jesus. "It is God's will that you should be sanctified: that you should avoid sexual immorality; that each of you should learn to control his own body in a way that is holy and honorable, not in passionate lust like the pagans, who do not know God" (1 Thess. 4:3–5).

This turnaround cannot happen without confessing all kinds of past sin. You have to know what they are in order to repent and be forgiven. Reread chapter 1, "How to Be Free from Guilt/How to Maintain Joy," or read one of these books: *The Calvary Road* by Roy Hession or *Continuous Revival* by Norman Grubb.

Of the sexual sins, pornography is the easiest sin to get out of because it only involves you. It may not seem easy, but that is because you have not hated it. Believe me, if there is another live person involved, either homosexual or heterosexual, it is much harder to break. There are all kinds of methods that work for getting rid of your pornography habit. There is one method that works permanently, and that is a complete surrender to the Savior.

If your sin is fornication, whether it is one time, with one woman or man, or if it is fifty people of the same sex or opposite sex, the solution is the same. If this activity has been normal to you, it is because you are not a Christian. When you receive Christ, all of this is forgiven.

If you are a Christian in this fornication, your conscience should be hurting very much. One obvious solution, if your partner is the opposite sex, is to marry the partner. However, if your partner is not a Christian, marrying is not a solution. "Do not be yoked together with unbelievers. For what do righteousness and wickedness have in common? Or what fellowship can light have with darkness? What harmony is there between

Christ and Belial? What does a believer have in common with an unbeliever? What agreement is there between the temple of God and idols? For we are the temple of the living God. As God has said: 'I will live with them and walk among them, and I will be their God, and they will be my people'" (2 Cor. 6:14–16). If your partner is not a Christian, you must break up the relationship, even if there is a child because of the relationship. Your partner is much more likely to become a Christian if you are separated and you have the joy of the Lord's salvation.

If it is adultery, break up. Confess to God. Confess to your spouse. Confess to the woman or man, confess to the other husband or wife if there is one, and confess to the church. If you are in a position of spiritual leadership, resign your position, even if it is your paid job.

The others might not forgive you. That is one of the consequences of sin.

Whatever your sexual sin, confession of sin and forsaking is the way. Look at the sin as it is: sin against God. "But in order that sin might be recognized as sin, it produced death in me through what was good, so that through the commandment sin might become *utterly sinful*" (Rom. 7:13b). It is utterly sinful. Hate it as God hates it.

One prevention for sexual sin is "do not touch." "Now concerning the things of which you wrote to me: It is good for a man not to touch a woman" (1 Cor. 7:1 NKJV). *Touching* in this context means to cause a sexual arousal. It does not necessarily even require physical contact.

The second prevention for sexual sin is marriage.

> But since there is so much immorality, each man should have his own wife, and each woman her own husband. The husband should fulfill his marital duty to his wife, and likewise the wife to her husband. The wife's body does not belong to her alone but also to her husband. In the same way, the husband's body does not belong to him alone but also to his wife. Do not deprive each other except by mutual consent and for a time, so that you may devote yourselves to prayer. Then come together again so that Satan will not tempt you because of your lack of self-control. (1 Cor. 7:2–5)

Fasting from sex is OK if the husband and wife agree about the fasting. Even then, it should not be for long, or Satan will tempt you with sex outside of marriage. I have known husbands and wives who withhold sex as punishment. *Do not do this.* Satan tempts them and often succeeds so that there is unfaithfulness on the part of the husband or wife. If sex is being withheld because of some other offense, that offense must be confessed and forgiven. This openness of confessing and forgiving should happen daily; don't put it off.

Another prevention for sexual sin is staying away from other, little sins. Psalm 19:13 tells us that Big Sin will not happen if willful sins do not control us. The great transgression will not come if you stay away from smaller sins. We will talk more about this in the final chapter.

CHAPTER 18

How to Be Free from Same-Sex Attraction

Many years ago, I counseled a fellow who was a virgin but was only attracted to men. I performed his wedding. Before his marriage, I encouraged him to tell his fiancée. He didn't want to. I said, "You have to tell her. She may not want to marry you." Later I visited them, and they had four sons. I don't know if he ever told her.

The world thinks that if we have an attraction to anyone of the opposite sex, we can express it anytime. The same happens with men who are attracted to men and women who are attracted to women. If it feels good, it must be OK.

Sexual attraction is part of our creation. However, simply being attracted to someone does not make it allowable to express that attraction outside of marriage. "Now concerning the things about which you wrote, it is good for a man not to touch a woman. But because of immoralities, each man is to have his own wife, and each woman is to have her own husband" (1 Cor. 7:1–2 NASB).

When a person is heterosexual, being attracted to the opposite sex does not mean you have the freedom to act on the attraction. You must still do it only within marriage. Likewise, having homosexual tendencies does not free you to practice homosexuality. You must still obey God's moral law.

Let's look at the biblical requirements related to this subject.

> As the sun was setting, Abram fell into a deep sleep, and a thick and dreadful darkness came over him. Then the LORD said to him, "Know for certain that your descendants will be strangers in a country not their own, and they will be enslaved and mistreated four hundred years. But I will punish the nation they serve as slaves, and afterward they will come out with great possessions. You, however, will go to your fathers in peace and be buried at a good old age. In the fourth generation your descendants will come back here, for the sin of the Amorites has not yet reached its full measure." (Gen. 15:12–16)

Abraham was born in Ur of the Chaldees. God promised the land of Canaan to his descendants, but He said that they could not have it for another four hundred years because the Amorites were not bad enough yet for Him to kick them out.

Another city nearby had reached the full measure of their sin.

> The two angels arrived at Sodom in the evening, and Lot was sitting in the gateway of the city. When he saw them, he got up to meet them and bowed down with his face to the ground. "My lords," he said, "please turn aside to your servant's house. You can wash your feet and spend the night and then go on your way early in the morning."
>
> "No," they answered, "we will spend the night in the square."
>
> But he insisted so strongly that they did go with him and entered his house. He prepared a meal for them, baking bread without yeast, and they ate. Before they had gone to bed, all the men from every part of the city of Sodom—both young and old—surrounded the house. They called to Lot, "Where are the men who came to you tonight? Bring them out to us so that we can have sex with them."
>
> Lot went outside to meet them and shut the door behind him and said, "No, my friends. Don't do this wicked thing. Look, I have two daughters who have never slept with a man. Let me bring them out

to you, and you can do what you like with them. But don't do anything to these men, for they have come under the protection of my roof."

"Get out of our way," they replied. And they said, "This fellow came here as an alien, and now he wants to play the judge! We'll treat you worse than them." They kept bringing pressure on Lot and moved forward to break down the door.

But the men inside reached out and pulled Lot back into the house and shut the door. Then they struck the men who were at the door of the house, young and old, with blindness so that they could not find the door. (Gen. 19:1–11)

God destroyed Sodom and Gomorrah for this evil.

After God delivered Israel from Egypt, the Lord said to Moses, "Speak to the Israelites and say to them: 'I am the LORD your God. You must not do as they do in Egypt, where you used to live, and you must not do as they do in the land of Canaan, where I am bringing you. Do not follow their practices. You must obey my laws and be careful to follow my decrees. I am the LORD your God. Keep my decrees and laws, for the person who obeys them will live by them. I am the LORD'" (Lev. 18:2–5).

Following this command is a list of specific rules against incest, child sacrifice, and homosexuality. "Do not lie with a man as one lies with a woman; that is detestable" (Lev. 18:22). God tells the Israelites what would happen if they behaved this way:

Do not defile yourselves in any of these ways, because this is how the nations that I am going to drive out before you became defiled. Even the land was defiled; so I punished it for its sin, and the land vomited out its inhabitants. But you must keep my decrees and my laws. The native-born and the aliens living among you must not do any of these detestable things, for all these things were done by the people who lived in the land before you, and the land became defiled. And if you defile the land, it will vomit you out as it vomited out the nations that were before you. (Lev. 18:24–28)

Some people dismiss this instruction by saying, "Well, that's the Old Testament." The Old Testament is inspired. Unless the things in it are *repudiated* by or *fulfilled* in the New Testament, they still apply today. Some people claim that unless they are stated again in the New Testament, they do not apply. That is not true, and it is not defensible from Scripture.

There are several kinds of laws in the Old Testament: the moral law (the Ten Commandments), sacrificial laws, civil laws, and health laws. The sacrificial laws were fulfilled in the death and resurrection of Jesus Christ (see Hebrews 10:11–18). The civil law has been transferred to the governments of the nations. Jesus did away with the health laws in Matthew 15. When the Pharisees objected to His disciples eating with unwashed hands, He said, "Not what goes into the mouth defiles a man; but what comes out of the mouth, this defiles a man" (Matt. 15:11 NKJV). The principles behind the health laws still apply—we should still wash our hands before we eat, but not because it makes us holy—it just keeps us from dying from whatever germs we might have had on our hands.

That leaves the moral law. The Ten Commandments and the other commands related to morality have not been abrogated or altered. This law still applies. "Or do you not know that the unrighteous will not inherit the kingdom of God? Do not be deceived; neither fornicators, nor idolaters, nor adulterers, nor effeminate, nor homosexuals, nor thieves, nor the covetous, nor drunkards, nor revilers, nor swindlers, will inherit the kingdom of God. Such were some of you; but you were washed, but you were sanctified, but you were justified in the name of the Lord Jesus Christ and in the Spirit of our God" (1 Cor. 6:9–11 NASB).

Notice that those who practice these sins will not inherit the kingdom of God. Notice also that of the ten sins listed here, four are sexual, and two of those four are homosexual. Homosexuality is very common in unbelieving countries. It is the way people have lived in Muslim countries for a long time and the way they lived in ancient Greece, Sodom, Gomorrah, and Egypt. When people live away from God, society goes this way fast.

The key verse is verse 11: "Such were some of you; but you were washed, but you were sanctified, but you were justified in the name of the Lord Jesus Christ and in the Spirit of our God." Although they do not deserve the kingdom of God, some of them are made righteous in the name of the Lord Jesus.

Four hundred years after Abraham, the people of Canaan were evil enough for God to destroy them, and He did. How did their depravity get started? Paul tells us in Romans:

> The wrath of God is being revealed from heaven against all the godlessness and wickedness of men who suppress the truth by their wickedness, since what may be known about God is plain to them, because God has made it plain to them. For since the creation of the world God's invisible qualities—his eternal power and divine nature—have been clearly seen, being understood from what has been made, so that men are without excuse.
>
> For although they knew God, they neither glorified him as God nor gave thanks to him, but their thinking became futile and their foolish hearts were darkened. Although they claimed to be wise, they became fools and exchanged the glory of the immortal God for images made to look like mortal man and birds and animals and reptiles.
>
> Therefore God gave them over in the sinful desires of their hearts to sexual impurity for the degrading of their bodies with one another. They exchanged the truth of God for a lie, and worshiped

and served created things rather than the Creator—
who is forever praised. Amen.

Because of this, God gave them over to shameful
lusts. Even their women exchanged natural relations
for unnatural ones. In the same way the men also
abandoned natural relations with women and were
inflamed with lust for one another. Men committed
indecent acts with other men, and received in themselves the due penalty for their perversion.

Furthermore, since they did not think it worthwhile to retain the knowledge of God, he gave them
over to a depraved mind, to do what ought not to be
done. They have become filled with every kind of
wickedness, evil, greed and depravity. They are full
of envy, murder, strife, deceit and malice. They are
gossips, slanderers, God-haters, insolent, arrogant
and boastful; they invent ways of doing evil; they
disobey their parents; they are senseless, faithless,
heartless, ruthless. Although they know God's righteous decree that those who do such things deserve
death, they not only continue to do these very things
but also approve of those who practice them. (Rom.
1:18–32)

This kind of depravity is a degenerative sin slide,
and it starts with *bad theology*. Men did not want to retain God in their minds. "For although they knew God,
they neither glorified him as God nor gave thanks to
him" (v. 21). When people start changing the character

of God, they become more sinful. Their advanced state of sin is a direct result of their bad theology. The Old Testament and the New Testament are consistent in their view of this. The Old Testament specifies what kinds of acts are forbidden, and the New Testament tells us that those acts are the end result of trying to do away with God.

There are three consequences in this passage. The first is in verse 24. Men did not honor God as God; "Therefore God gave them over in the sinful desires of their hearts to sexual impurity for the degrading of their bodies with one another." The second: "since they did not think it worthwhile to retain the knowledge of God, he gave them over to a depraved mind, to do what ought not to be done" (v. 28). The third: "And although they know the ordinance of God, that those who practice such things are worthy of death, they not only do the same, but also give hearty approval to those who practice them" (v. 32). God gave them over to gross sin as a result of their refusal to worship Him.

If I had a choice of selling bad theology or pornography in a bookstore (and those were the only two choices), I would not sell bad theology. It is the worst. Pornography is bad, but bad theology *causes* pornography.

ENVIRONMENT AND NURTURE

The historical secular position is that sexual orientation is affected by environment and nurture. In his 1980 work *Overcoming Homosexuality*, clinical psychologist

Robert Kronemeyer wrote, "With rare exceptions, homosexuality is neither inherited nor the result of some glandular disturbance or the scrambling of genes or chromosomes. Homosexuals are made, not born 'that way.' I firmly believe that homosexuality is a learned response to early painful experiences and that it can be unlearned. For those homosexuals who are unhappy with their life and find effective therapy, it is 'curable.'"[15]

John DeCecco, former editor of the *Journal of Homosexuality*, says that homosexuality is "a behavior, not a condition," and something that some people can and do change.[16] Homosexuality does not happen by birth. Some men seem effeminate from childhood, and some women seem very masculine, but they are still men and still women. We are all created male or female with an attraction to the opposite sex.

How does this happen if people are not born that way? Speaking socially instead of religiously, here is how. The problem starts in the relationships within the home. Both sexes need love and respect, and they need it from both sexes of parents. A little boy who gets much love from his father and much love from his mother will grow up pretty normal. If a girl has much love from her mother and much love from her father, she grows up to be normal.

15. Robert Kronemeyer, *Overcoming Homosexuality*, p. 7 (New York: Macmillan Publishing Co., 1980)
16. Kim Painter, *A Biological Theory for Sexual Preference*, USA Today, 1 January 1989, p. 4D

If, however, the boy spends all his time with his dad, and his mother is not very affectionate toward him, he will be looking for female attention very early in life. When guys in junior high are being very aggressive toward the girls, it is not because they have had too much masculine attention; they have not had enough feminine attention. It is the same way with girls. If her father pays no attention to her when she is growing up, she will start looking for male attention. These two people find each other in junior high. They are both starved for attention from the opposite sex, and they glom onto each other because of it. Sex is the result, but it is not the real need.

Now consider a situation where there is a son and a daughter in the same home, and the father shows love to both children, but the mother doesn't give adequate attention to either of them. The son and the daughter will both look for female attention outside the home. The son becomes heterosexually promiscuous, and the daughter becomes a lesbian. Both children go astray for exactly the same reason—not getting enough love from their mother. They needed more female attention.

Suppose the father doesn't give attention to either. The daughter looks for male attention, and the son looks for male attention. The boy does not plan to become homosexual, and the girl does not plan to be promiscuous. It is not their intent; it is just their *need*.

I used to travel regularly to speak at conferences. When I did, I would stay with Christian families.

Normally, while I was waiting for supper, I would pay attention to the children. If I said to a little girl, "Come and sit in Uncle Jim's lap," and she grabbed her father's leg and held on tight, I knew it was a good home. If she ran and jumped in my lap, that did not mean it was a bad home. But if three hours later I was still trying to scoot her off my lap, I knew it was a bad home, because that told me she was hungry for male attention.

In one case like that, I told the mother that her little girl was looking for male attention.

"Oh yes," she said, "She hugs the mailman, the milkman, and anyone else who comes to the house."

She was starved for it. She was an adopted daughter. The natural affection wasn't there, and the adoptive parents didn't work at it enough. (What I didn't realize at the time was that the mother wasn't getting any attention from the husband, either.) That girl was pregnant by the time she was seventeen and later moved in with a lesbian. She didn't get attention from her father or her mother, and she was looking for love.

It is easy for a father to think, "I am going to raise my boys to be very masculine," not realizing that by putting an emphasis on that, he might be raising them to be the opposite. Boys need hugs from their father so that they will not have that emptiness, that crying need for male affection. "I don't want my boys to grow up to be sissies, so I'll teach them to be hard." No. They are little kids. Children of both sexes are still children. What they need is a great deal of attention and affection.

The more secure a man or boy is at home, the less he will need a woman. The closer a woman is with her father, the less she needs a man. They still have a sexual drive, but they do not have an inordinate need for sex because they are not starved for attention. In fact, one of the best ways for guys to stay single longer (so you're not aching to be married at the age of fifteen) is to have a good friendship and spend time with your sisters and your mother.

I was determined that this problem would not happen to my family. I decided that when I went home each night, I would pour it on my kids. One time, when my daughter Heather was a senior in high school, I went up to tuck her in bed and kiss her goodnight.

She said, "Dad, I know why you're doing this."

"Why?"

"You're afraid I'm going to get my loving someplace else."

I said, "Right on!"

This is something that you must teach your children about and protect them from. The best prevention is teaching them a very high view of God and giving much love from both sexes of parents to both sexes of children. Keep it up, even right through junior high when your sons will tell you to lay off. Do it anyhow. It is better to make them say, "Oh, that dumb Mom," than to have them think they are not loved.

The more secure a person is, the less they will be pulled toward sexual relationships outside of marriage. If you have that emptiness, that hunger, you are ready for someone to take advantage of you, and there are many people out there who are willing to do it.

Many, many people get approached by someone of the same sex. My wife was a missionary with the Women's Union Missionary Society in Japan when we got married. She could not leave her post right away, because there was no one to replace her as principal of the Bible school. The board of her mission was all-female. The missionaries were female doctors, female nurses, and female teachers ministering in India, China, and Japan in women's Bible schools, women's hospitals, and women's schools. It was a women's mission to women. The woman they sent to succeed Bessie as principal of the Bible school had very high recommendations. She was a lesbian. When it was found out, she was told to leave immediately, but before that, she approached Bessie.

When I was sixteen and seventeen, I worked in the stockyards of Omaha, Nebraska. Looking back now, I suppose most of the men who were still there and not off fighting in the war were homosexual. It never occurred to me at the time. But I remember some of the things they said to me. One guy who was married and had several children invited me to go to the movies with him. I said, "I'll ask my parents." My parents said no. What was a thirty-five-year-old guy wanting to take a sixteen-year-old kid to the movies for? At the time, I didn't even know there was such a thing as homosexuality. That's probably what kept me OK—I was so dumb!

When I lived in Annapolis, I had a friend who was an engineering professor. His brother was a harpist and was offered a scholarship to Juilliard. Their father was travelling through Annapolis on his way to New York City to find a place for his son to stay. The professor asked me to see the father. I told him not to let his son go to Juilliard.

"Why?"

"All the men are gay."

He couldn't comprehend that. He found a place for his son to live, and the son went up to school. On his first day, he returned home to find two guys kissing each other on the floor outside his room, and he thought, "I'm getting out of here!"

I had another friend named Frances Simpson who was an interior decorator in New York City. She said that every male interior decorator she knew in New York City was homosexual. That was fifty years ago.

If you do not have trouble in this area, you do not need to be afraid because homosexuality is so common. Just walk closely with the Lord, and these things will not be a temptation to you. In fact, you may be able to have a good witness to people who are this way.

These relationships often start out as nothing more than friendships. Once a relationship becomes physical, the sex drive takes over. Suppose a college student is having sex with as many women as he can. That might be a few dozen women. But if the same guy is homosexual, he can have encounters with hundreds of men. They have "anonymous sex." It becomes an obsession. The need for the physical act of sex is far greater with homosexuals than it is with heterosexuals. This does not mean that heterosexual people are necessarily more moral (they're not), but the obsession is stronger in the homosexual community. Sex itself is dominant.

Homosexual relations can also happen the same way they happen heterosexually: people who are otherwise well-balanced go off to college and get drunk. If a girl gets drunk, either some guy takes her to bed, or some woman takes her to bed, and that starts it.

CAUSES: MEN AND WOMEN

As we have already discussed, the basic reason for homosexual attraction is not knowing the Father through the Son; having a wrong view of God is the way this sets itself up in society. The secondary reason for homosexual attraction is inadequate love and affection from your parents. There are several other events that can lead to a homosexual lifestyle.

For men, these factors can include the following:

- When a boy is starved for male affection, an older male student, teacher, or relative can fill the gap in his need for love. Sometimes it is good and normal, but often it is not. If it is pleasant, the boy wants more. Because he had this experience with a man and liked it, he thinks that is the way it should be.

- In puberty, he goes through sex education classes telling him not to get involved with the opposite sex. As a result, he keeps away from girls, but he hasn't been warned about the same sex, so he does not have his guard up with them. Then someone will be physically friendly in the locker room.

- He is training his mind. The brain controls actions, but repeated actions can train the brain. If a child's brain is not working to train him to crawl, his parents can move his legs to teach him. That action trains his brain. It is the same with this kind of homosexual action. Practice trains him to think of it as normal.

Things that can lead to a homosexual lifestyle for women include the following:

- Female friends at school. One or two will be really nice to her, not because they are Christians, but because they are out to seduce her.

- She has been raped by a family member or neighbor. No action has been taken, so she begins to hate men (not just the men who raped her, but the men in the family who did not protect her or go after the rapist).

- She is attracted to masculine women. Initially, the masculine women will be kind. After they have convinced her that she belongs to the dominant woman, that woman becomes a crutch. It starts out with just an attraction, and it becomes sensual, sexual, physical.

- She marries a man and finds out that he is not kind or loving. She remembers the women who were kind to her and starts looking for one.

- She enlists in the armed forces. Homosexuality is a great problem in the military. As long as women have been in the military, lesbians have been going there to be where the women are. It does not take long for a female drill sergeant to seduce her. There will also be hundreds of sailors/soldiers looking for an easy mark. She can go down in both directions. She will hate the men more than she hates the women: the men are looking for one-night stands, but the women will want her permanently. She may not know how to explain why she feels what she feels.

GETTING OUT

How do you get out? If you are not a Christian, the best way out is to receive Christ as Lord. Find a Christian you respect and ask him how and why he became a Christian. If you are a woman, find a Christian woman or family who will take you in and love you into the kingdom. Become friends with women you do not think of sexually.

Read your Bible, beginning with Luke, John, Acts, and Romans. As you apply what you read, your eyes will open. You will be able to see light, and you will be attracted to it.

Confess to God any sin in your thought life or actions. Confess to Him any part you played in sexual events that happened to you early in life, then thank Him for His forgiveness.

> For God so loved the world, that He gave His only begotten Son, that whoever believes in Him shall not perish, but have eternal life. (John 3:16 NKJV)

> Truly, truly, I say to you, he who hears My word, and believes Him who sent Me, has eternal life, and does not come into judgment, but has passed out of death into life. (John 5:24 NASB)

> He saved us, not on the basis of deeds which we have done in righteousness, but according to His mercy, by the washing of regeneration and renewing by the Holy Spirit, whom He poured out upon us richly through Jesus Christ our Savior, so that being justified by His grace we would be made heirs according to the hope of eternal life. This is a trustworthy statement; and concerning these things I want you to speak confidently, so that those who have believed God will be careful to engage in good deeds. These things are good and profitable for men. (Titus 3:5–8 NASB)

When you say yes to God, your life will change immediately. You will have a clean and sensitive conscience. You will want to be with real Christians. You will start to see your same-sex attraction as sin.

Get rid of all pornography.

If you are living in a homosexual relationship, your relationship will have to end. Life in Christ does not allow sexual relationships outside of marriage.

If you are a Christian and are attracted to the opposite sex, do not act on that attraction or respond to anyone who approaches you. Pray that God will fix it. You were not born with this attraction. It was learned, and it can be unlearned. Ask God to help you unlearn it.

FOR PARENTS WHO HAVE A HOMOSEXUAL CHILD

Do not write them off. They need you very much.

Realize that you may have contributed to this lifestyle by not expressing love to them when they were growing up.

Confess the sin of not loving them, then choose to love them.

Decide to express love many ways. *Do not give up.*

Continue to love them until they want to be like you.

Many men and women who are committed to a homosexual lifestyle insist that they were that way from birth. There is no conclusive evidence of a biological cause for homosexuality, and there is much evidence of the heterosexual nature of the child from birth. The child has been trained for homosexual attraction by lack of attention, abuse, teaching, and/or being taken advantage of. This can be cured by the gospel, and training and teaching can be reversed by the child and those close to him or her. If your child is in this situation, please read my booklet *How to Lead Your Wayward Children Back to the Lord.*[17]

> Do you not know that the wicked will not inherit the kingdom of God? Do not be deceived: Neither the sexually immoral nor idolaters nor adulterers nor male prostitutes nor homosexual offenders nor thieves nor the greedy nor drunkards nor slanderers nor swindlers will inherit the kingdom of God. And that is what some of you were. But you were washed, you were sanctified, you were justified in the name of the Lord Jesus Christ and by the Spirit of our God. (1 Cor. 6:9–11)

Paul is very explicit: God delivers people from this. Ask Him to deliver you.

17. Available at ccmbooks.org.

CHAPTER 19

How to Walk in the Light

> This is the message we have heard from him and declare to you: God is light; in him there is no darkness at all. (1 John 1:5)

*E*ven in a well-lit room, there are shadows. Outside it is brighter, but there is darkness out there, too. As I look out the window from my desk, I see an apple tree with six inches of snow on each branch. That tree is "white as snow," but even it is in darkness because the sky is overcast. David prayed in Psalm 51:7, "Cleanse me with hyssop, and I will be clean; wash me, and I will be whiter than snow." God is light, and in Him there is *no darkness at all.*

"But if we walk in the light, as he is in the light, we have fellowship with one another, and the blood of Jesus, his Son, purifies us from all sin" (1 John 1:7). The word *purifies* means "keeps on cleansing." It is a continuous washing. Walking in the light means that as soon as you sin, you are aware of it, you confess it, and it gets cleansed. The result? We have fellowship with one another. Walking in the light does not mean never sinning, but it does mean that obedience is your normal state of being.

"We proclaim to you what we have seen and heard so that you also may have fellowship with us. And our fellowship is with the Father and with His Son Jesus Christ" (1 John 1:3). When we are walking in the light, we also have fellowship with God.

This book has given you instruction on how to be free from various sins. Now your goal is to stay free. That means staying cleansed from sin, and in order to get that cleansing, you need to know when you have sinned. You are most likely to notice your sin when you are in the light.

In the year that King Uzziah died, I saw the Lord seated on a throne, high and exalted, and the train of his robe filled the temple. Above him were seraphs, each with six wings: With two wings they covered their faces, with two they covered their feet, and with two they were flying. And they were calling to one another:

"Holy, holy, holy is the LORD Almighty;
the whole earth is full of his glory."

At the sound of their voices the doorposts and thresholds shook and the temple was filled with smoke.

"Woe to me!" I cried. "I am ruined! For I am a man of unclean lips, and I live among a people of unclean lips, and my eyes have seen the King, the LORD Almighty."

Then one of the seraphs flew to me with a live coal in his hand, which he had taken with tongs from the altar. With it he touched my mouth and said, "See, this has touched your lips; your guilt is taken away and your sin atoned for." (Isa. 6:1–7)

In the presence of complete light, Isaiah saw his sinfulness, confessed, and was cleansed immediately.

How do you walk in the light? First, *confess every sin to God as soon as you are aware of it.* "If we confess our sins, he is faithful and just and will forgive us our sins and purify us from all unrighteousness" (1 John 1:9). God forgives the sins we confess to Him, and He forgives them right away. This cleanses us whiter than snow and gets us back into the light.

Often, we sin for a while, get clean, sin for a while, get clean, sin for a while . . . That is the method of the average Christian. That is not walking in the light! Walking in the light continually cleanses. When we make a habit of keeping short accounts with God, it becomes more natural to be obedient. When we disobey, we are brought up short right away, and the sin gets cleansed right away.

The Scripture says, "Light has come into the world, but men loved darkness instead of light because their deeds were evil. Everyone who does evil hates the light, and will not come into the light for fear that his deeds will be exposed. But whoever lives by the truth comes into the light, so that it may be seen plainly that what he has done has been done through God" (John 3:19–21). When you walk in the light, you are *asking* to be reproved. Some children do everything to hide what they have done wrong. Others do everything to get caught. They want to be corrected. God wants us to be the kind of people who *want* to get caught.

The trouble is that when you are in sin, you won't want to come to the light. The solution? Program yourself ahead of time for what you will do when you get into sin.

Suppose I am in flight training, and there's a red handle in the cockpit marked *Eject*. I don't practice pulling the red handle. But I program my head so that if the wrong lights go on or there's smoke in the cockpit, I don't need to stop and debate with myself about what to do. I pull the red handle! I am trained to eject in certain situations.

When things are going well, program yourself to say, "Turn to the light; turn to the light; turn to the light." When something goes wrong, that training will tell you to turn back to God.

Another aspect of walking in the light is *spending time with the Lord every single day in the Word and in prayer*. We will look at prayer first.

Get into the habit of praying. I am not a very good prayer when it comes to setting aside time and praying for an hour straight. I am much better at praying all the time. If I'm walking, running, or sitting, if I'm driving, if I'm thinking, I talk to God.

Mostly I talk about people. I don't talk to God about myself much, unless I'm in trouble. Years ago, InterVarsity staff member Bill Steeper said, "It was a wonderful thing when I got myself off my own hands." He turned himself over to God.

Corrie ten Boom said the same thing to me. She was riding in the back of a car one night on a dangerous road. The driver was going way too fast, and she was terrified. She decided to spend the time interceding for other people. When she prayed for others, her fear disappeared.

And so it was, after the LORD had spoken these words to Job, that the LORD said to Eliphaz the Temanite, "My wrath is aroused against you and your two friends, for you have not spoken of Me what is right, as My servant Job has. Now therefore, take for yourselves seven bulls and seven rams, go to My servant Job, and offer up for yourselves a burnt offering; and My servant Job shall pray for you. For I will accept him, lest I deal with you according to your folly; because you have not spoken of Me what is right, as My servant Job has." So Eliphaz the Temanite and Bildad the Shuhite and Zophar the Naamathite went and did as the LORD commanded them; for the LORD had accepted Job. *And the Lord restored Job's losses when he prayed for his friends.* Indeed the LORD gave Job twice as much as he had before. (Job 42:7–10 NKJV)

Job had repented, and the Lord had accepted him, but it was when Job interceded for his friends that the Lord acted to restore his fortunes. Make it a habit to intercede for others every day. No family is without problems. My family has had our share of them. What has helped us most is not letting ourselves get wrapped up in the problems. When we keep interceding for and being concerned about others, we don't have time to be too concerned about ourselves.

One of the first times I spoke on this subject was after the birth and death of our little granddaughter Alexa. My daughter-in-law Meredith was two weeks overdue. Alexa was 9 lbs. 10 oz., the labor was long, and she was born not breathing. Two of the nurses were in tears. Meredith was comforting one nurse, and my son Gordon was comforting the other. That's the way it was for the next fifteen months until Alexa died. When you give yourself to other people, God gives you extra grace for your own troubles.

You need to make a choice. Choose to always turn up to God; don't ever turn inward. Turning inward is a downhill spiral.

"Doubtless," said I, "what it utters is its only stock and store

Caught from some unhappy master whom unmer-
    ciful Disaster
Followed fast and followed faster till his songs one
    burden bore—
Till the dirges of his Hope that melancholy burden bore
Of 'Never—nevermore.'"[18]

Do not turn in! Turn up to the light and turn out
to others. When you look *up* instead of in, you will become
aware of your sin, but once you are aware of it, it can be
taken care of right away. You will be back in the joy of
the Lord quickly. When you look out, you will be concerned about others, for their benefit.

Next, *spend time in the Word.* "The Bible will keep
you from sin, or sin will keep you from the Bible."[19]

The law of the LORD is perfect, converting the soul;
The testimony of the LORD is sure, making wise the
    simple;
The statutes of the LORD are right, rejoicing the heart;
The commandment of the LORD is pure, enlighten-
    ing the eyes;
The fear of the LORD is clean, enduring forever;
The judgments of the LORD are true and righteous
    altogether.
More to be desired are they than gold,

18.   Edgar Allan Poe, "*The Raven.*"
19.   Dwight L. Moody

Yea, than much fine gold;
Sweeter also than honey and the honeycomb.
Moreover by them Your servant is warned,
And in keeping them there is great reward.
Who can understand his errors?
Cleanse me from secret faults.
Keep back Your servant also from presumptuous
    sins;
Let them not have dominion over me.
Then I shall be blameless,
And I shall be innocent of great transgression.
Let the words of my mouth and the meditation of
    my heart
Be acceptable in Your sight,
O LORD, my strength and my Redeemer.
(Psalm 19:7–14 NKJV)

The law of the Lord is perfect, and it converts the soul. God's revelation revives, awakens, and changes men. His Word makes us wise, it rejoices, it enlightens, it endures.

When you read the Word, do you have a sense that you are immersed in something that is perfect, right, sure, clean, and righteous altogether? Are you enraptured by it? The Psalmist was. "More to be desired are they than gold, yea, than much fine gold" (v. 10). He desired God's Word for wealth—perfect wealth, fine gold. "Sweeter also than honey and the honeycomb" (v. 10). He desired it for taste—a pleasure he genuinely enjoyed.

Do you desire the Word of God like you desire wealth? Do you desire it like you desire honey? Does it taste sweet to you? We should have a great desire for the Word of God.

There have been times in my life when I would read the Word, and it seemed rather dead—and other times when I just couldn't get enough of it in quantity or in quality. I would be so wrapped up in it that I wouldn't know whether to go on to the next passage or go back and repeat. I wanted more, and I also didn't want to lose what I'd just gotten, because it was so precious, so sweet, so wonderful. It really revives the soul, it really makes wise the simple, it really rejoices the heart, it really enlightens the eyes.

What else does God's revelation do? "Moreover by them Your servant is warned" (v. 11). It warns us. "And in keeping them there is great reward" (v. 11). When we obey these testimonies from God, there is great reward.

"Who can understand his errors? Cleanse me from secret faults" (v. 12). For most of my life, I assumed that "secret faults" were sins that I wasn't aware of, and that we are to use this as a prayer of general confession after we have confessed the sins we know. Then I was spending time in *The Treasury of David* (Spurgeon's commentary on the Psalms), and I found that very few people thought that. They said it meant, "Keep me from hiding my sins," the way David tried to hide his. Of course, there is no sense in trying to hide the sins we do openly—everyone knows about them already.

Certain sins we do privately: things we think, things we say. Those are harder to confess—just the fact that we hid them in the first place means we don't want to acknowledge them, because that would require bringing them out into the open before God. The psalmist asks God to expose the things he is hiding. That had happened to him. When David thought he had hidden his sin of adultery and murder, it took the prophet Nathan to tell him a parable and bring it out into the open.

Hiding sin is deadly. We might think nobody knows about it, and nobody's going to know. We end up deceiving ourselves. There was a poem written in the 1800s about a man who murdered someone and buried him in a deep, dark stream. He went back the next day and found that the stream bed had gone dry, and there lay the corpse out in the open. He covered the corpse with leaves, and the wind blew them away. He realized that even if he buried the body ten thousand fathoms deep, he wasn't going to get away with the murder.

> Down went the corse with hollow plunge
>   And vanish'd in the pool;
> Anon I cleans'd my bloody hands,
>   And wash'd my forehead cool,
> And sat among the urchins young,
>   That evening in the school.
>   .   .   .   .
> Heavily I rose up, as soon
>   As light was in the sky,

And sought the black accursed pool
   With a wild misgiving eye:
And I saw the Dead in the river bed,
   For the faithless stream was dry.

. . . .

With breathless speed, like a soul in chase,
   I took him up and ran;
There was no time to dig a grave
   Before the day began:
In a lonesome wood, with heaps of leaves,
   I hid the murder'd man.

And all that day I read in school,
   But my thought was other where;
As soon as the mid-day task was done,
   In secret I was there;
And a mighty wind had swept the leaves,
   And still the corse was bare!

Then down I cast me on my face,
   And first began to weep,
For I knew my secret then was one
   That earth refus'd to keep:
Or land or sea, though he should be
   Ten thousand fathoms deep.

So wills the fierce avenging Sprite,
   Till blood for blood atones!
Aye, though he 's buried in a cave,
   And trodden down with stones,

And years have rotted off his flesh,—
The world shall see his bones.[20]

Lord, cleanse Thou me from the things I am hiding. "Who can understand his errors?" (v. 12). We may not understand our own sin because of our remarkable ability to self-deceive. The Word of God reveals our errors.

"Keep back Your servant also from presumptuous sins" (v. 13). A presumptuous sin is something that you have *not* deceived yourself about. You knew it was wrong, but you had the audacity to do it anyway. By man's valuation, it may not be a very big sin, but it is deliberate—for instance, a white lie. We dare to lie, and God tells us that He has prepared a lake of fire for all liars. We dare to lie, and the Word says God hates liars. We don't hide presumptuous sins; we pull them off because everyone else is doing them, too. David asks God to keep him away from such sin.

"Let them not have dominion over me" (v. 13). I do it, I know it is wrong, and I do it again, and again, and again. Pretty soon, this sin has me in a vise. It has power over me, and I cannot keep from doing it. It may be an "acceptable" sin because everyone else is presuming it, too. But unless I am kept back from it, I end up as its slave. Let them not have dominion over me.

"Then I shall be blameless, and I shall be innocent of great transgression" (v. 13). I counsel many people who have committed great transgressions. They

20. Thomas Hood, "The Dream of Eugene Aram."

confess the sin, and God forgives them—and they turn right around and do it again. They confess it again, and they do it again. One man came to me for help with this. He would commit the sin, confess it, be forgiven, and immediately he would be right back in temptation. He would fall over the cliff again, confess, and find himself tottering on the edge once more. He asked me, "Why do I keep doing this when I have confessed it each time?"

If he would take care of his other sins, he would be far away from the edge. The reason people keep doing big sins over and over is that they have not been delivered from the presumptuous sins and the secret sins that led up to them. The man who keeps falling is confessing his great sins, but he isn't confessing his little ones.

When people file for divorce, generally the situation is so bad, and they hate each other so much, that it seems like there is no way to correct it. They did not anticipate this when they got married. If they had been kept from secret sins and presumptuous sins, the divorce would never have happened.

The way to stay away from big sins is to stay away from little ones. Don't put up with *any* sin in yourself. Keep your little sins confessed so that they cannot get dominion over you. I don't have to worry about ever committing a great transgression if I am kept from minor ones. If I am constantly confessing the secret sins and the presumptuous sins, the devil can't get close to me on a big one. He won't even try.

People have often asked me why I never have any big sin problems and why my family isn't messed up like many other families. Simple. We take care of the secret sins and the presumptuous ones. It's not that we're favored. We aren't. The devil simply knows that he can't trip us up with great temptations, so he works on us with little ones (or he keeps trying to, anyway). He knows he cannot get us into the eighth grade in sin until we pass the first grade. As long as I keep flunking the devil's first grade, I get held back, and I don't make it to his advanced courses. Make sure you are flunking the devil's first grade.

"Let the words of my mouth and the meditation of my heart be acceptable in Thy sight, O Lord, my Rock and my Redeemer" (v. 14). Many people, even Christians, don't particularly care what they say in public or to whom they say it. Some of us care very much. We think that if we pass the public approval on what we say, we're OK.

David wasn't satisfied with that. He said, "Let the words of my mouth and the meditation of my heart be acceptable in *Your* sight, O God." When we ask the Lord to make what we think about in our hearts and say with our mouths acceptable in *His* sight, not just in other people's sight, we don't have to worry about any great transgression.

We can pass this to our children as well. We are used to laying out rules for them to make their actions acceptable in our sight. Suppose we could teach our children so that the meditation of their hearts would be acceptable in the sight of God? If our children were like that, how many rules would we have to lay down? Not many. Not many at all.

Here is how you can teach your children to meditate on the Lord and have their meditation be acceptable in His sight. First, keep *your* meditation acceptable in God's sight and the words of *your* mouth acceptable in His sight. How do you speak to your children? Is that how you speak to everyone else? The Scripture says, "Out of the abundance of the heart the mouth speaks" (Matt. 12:34 NKJV). When I take care of the meditation of my heart, I have already taken care of what I'm going to say. What you say is the result of what you're meditating on. If you are not meditating rightly, what you say will not be right either in content or in manner. Your children will pick it up and meditate right back to you that way.

James 3 says that out of the same mouth proceed blessing and cursing, and that should not be. Ask God to make the meditation of your heart acceptable in His sight. That is the solution for holy, godly contact. That is where to start. Start with *your* heart, *your* motivation. Then you can go on to your children's hearts, your children's motivations.

Go back to dealing with secret sins. Go back to presumptuous sins. Go back to the words of your mouth and the meditations of your heart. When you get those things acceptable in God's sight, you won't have to worry about falling over any cliffs.

It is easy to fixate on big sins and let anything less than them pass for OK. You are doing something little that is not right, and someone says, "What's wrong with that?" That's what wrong with it—*saying*, "What's wrong with it." What's wrong is wanting to say that anything less than a big sin is OK.

We live as if sin were the same as crime. If it's not violating the law, then it's alright. If it's not *literally* violating the Ten Commandments, it's OK. But Jesus said that "anyone who looks at a woman lustfully has already committed adultery with her in his heart" (Matt. 5:28). God is after the meditation of your heart. The person who solves the problem there doesn't have to worry about the act of adultery. The person who solves the problem of hatred never has to worry about murder. The person who solves the problem of coveting never has to worry about stealing. Go after the basic things. Go after the heart sins underneath.

What if you are already guilty of the basic things? God forgives those like He forgives great transgressions. But you have to admit it first. You have to call it sin. You may have a good reputation with your friends and family, but you are miserable in your heart. If so, start asking God to search your heart.

Recently I reread a letter I received in the 1970s from the wife of a Navy captain of the Naval Academy Class of '53. Her husband had just told her that that as soon as the seniors of the class of 1950 graduated at the end of his plebe year, the plebes (the freshmen) went through all the seniors' rooms to see if they had left anything behind.

This man was not a Christian. He was searching through the dorms, and he came to my room. He pulled open the locker door, and on the inside panel was pasted Psalm 139:9: "If I take the wings of the morning, and dwell in the uttermost parts of the sea, even there Thy hand shall lead me, and Thy right hand shall hold me." That struck him. He became a Christian shortly thereafter, and twenty-six years later, I found out that that verse of Scripture pasted up in my locker door had helped bring him to the Lord.

Psalm 139 is the greatest cure there is for secret sins. It is the story of a man trying to run away from God and not succeeding. Verse 23 says, "Search me, O God, and know my heart. Try me and know my thoughts, and see if there be any wicked way in me, and lead me in the way everlasting." If you don't know what the problem is, ask God to search you. Then in prevention of future sin, ask Him to cause the meditation of your heart to be acceptable in His sight.

Look back at Psalm 19. David's great desire and delight came from the Word of God. The Word of God is light; the Word of God is a joy. If you do not know how to meditate in an acceptable way, dwell in the Scriptures, and you will come to find them like gold, like much fine gold. Your heart will change directly proportional to how much time you spend in the Word of God.

The last aspect of walking in the light that I will mention here is *being thankful*. This will help with *many* areas of your life. Start by recognizing that God is the Creator of all things. Look at all the trees, all the flowers, all the clouds, stars, sun, and moon. Thank God. Then thank God for all of your family. Thank Him for everything you have.

> Give thanks in all circumstances; for this is God's will for you in Christ Jesus. (1 Thess. 5:18)

> Do not be anxious about anything, but in everything, by prayer and petition, with thanksgiving, present your requests to God. And the peace of God, which transcends all understanding, will guard your hearts and your minds in Christ Jesus. (Phil. 4:6–7)

Giving thanks is God's will for you. It results in peace that passes all comprehension.

> I have not stopped giving thanks for you, remembering you in my prayers. (Eph. 1:16)

> I thank my God every time I remember you. In all my prayers for all of you, I always pray with joy because of your partnership in the gospel from the first day until now, being confident of this, that he who began a good work in you will carry it on to completion until the day of Christ Jesus. (Phil. 1:3–6)

Being thankful is an exercise of the will in obeying God's command to be thankful in everything. The Scripture does not say, "Be thankful *for* everything." Be thankful *in* everything. I am not thankful *for* being sick, but I can be thankful *in* being sick. When I am thankful in everything, then I can rejoice always. When I make my petitions to God with thankfulness, I end up with peace.

One of the signs of walking in the light is *singing*. This is not a way to walk in the light, but a result of it. When you walk in the light, you may end up singing to the Lord, even if you don't know any great hymns.

I knew one young woman who had been "converted" several times and still wasn't saved. She had read every book in the Christian bookstore and gone to every counselor in town. She went to multiple people for counseling, attended our school of practical Christianity, and read several books. I met with her and her husband a couple times and with her more times. She knew all the answers but did not seem able to put them into effect in her life.

One day she showed up at our front door. Bessie met her and told her to go sit in one of the chairs under the apple tree in the backyard while she went to find me.

At that moment, I was reading a book by Watchman Nee, and I had just read a paragraph where Nee said (to paraphrase), "Two men can hear the same text preached at the same time. 'I am the way the truth and the life; no man cometh to the Father but by me.' One person will hear that text and say, 'Oh, that's wonderful!' and will come to the Father through Jesus Christ. Another person will say, 'Oh, what a wonderful doctrine!' and come to the doctrine."

Having just read that paragraph, I quoted it to the young woman under the apple tree. She asked me, "What is the difference between the two?"

I said, "The first has love, joy, and peace, and the other has a plaque on the wall."

The next day she called to tell me that she was not a Christian. I replied that I did not think she was, either. She got upset with me because I agreed with her.

I told her that I would not tell her how to become a Christian. Her head was filled with the gospel already. If I told her, she would go through the motions and not be any more saved afterward. I said, "I'm not going to tell you how to become a Christian, because you are a doer, and you'd just go plug the formula. You've plugged it several times already, and nothing's happened. If I tell you how to come to the Father, you won't understand it. Grace, love, faith: all these terms you know by heart are empty words to you. There are certain things you need to find out for yourself first. You have to find out that God is holy. You have to find out how awfully sinful you are. You have to find out how great the love of God is. After you have some glimmer of the holiness of God, and after you have some small understanding of how sinful you are in the light of that holiness, and after you begin to see how much love God has for you in your sinfulness, then I will tell you the good news."

I did not hear from her for several weeks. Then she called and asked, "How could the Father love the Son and send Him to the cross?" She was starting to understand. "Oh!" I replied. "It didn't say He loved the Son. It says, 'For God so loved the *world* that He gave His only begotten Son.' That tells us not how much He loves the Son, but how much He loves the world."

I realized that she probably had enough understanding for me to tell her the gospel. However, I wanted to speak to her heart. Her head was already filled with truth, but it had not sunk in. I decided to give her the gospel in song and poetry. Over the phone, I sang her hymns like *The Love of God, The Deep, Deep Love of Jesus,* and *At Calvary.*

Sometime later, she was working a job cleaning apartments. As she ran the vacuum, she was singing, "He is Lord, He is Lord, He has risen from the dead, and He is Lord," and she was saved in the middle of the chorus. She was looking up to God, and her conversion was real.

Walking in the light is a grace and faith event. There is no other way. Colossians 2:6 (ESV) says, "Therefore, as you received Christ Jesus the Lord, so walk in Him." How did you receive Christ Jesus the Lord? By effort? By trying? No. You quit trying when you received Christ Jesus the Lord, and you trusted. When you quit trying and trusted grace, the Lord changed your life.

"Therefore, as you received Christ Jesus the Lord, so walk in Him." The same procedure by which I was saved is the way I live the Christian life. When I became a Christian, I quit trying—and having become one, I still quit trying. Living the Christian life is like being born again every instant. It's grace and faith. You didn't try to get in, and you don't try to live.

You say, "Yes, I do."

Well, tell me this: do you succeed?

People come to me and say, "Jim, I don't know why I failed. I *tried* to live the Christian life."

"Oh," I say, "that's why. You fell because you tried to live the Christian life."

We are not to try to live the Christian life. Walking in the light is grace, faith, grace, faith. As soon as we get saved, we are tempted to revert to trying. We are not to do that. The entire book of Galatians was written against that. Paul said, "Oh foolish Galatians!" (Gal. 3:1). You idiots! Tell me how you got into this kingdom. "Did you receive the Spirit by the works of the law, or by the hearing of faith? Are you so foolish? Having been made alive by the Spirit, are you now made perfect by the flesh?" (Gal. 6:2–3).

Look up to God and reject trying. This is what the New Testament teaches. We read it and hear something else. We try to reinterpret everything into something we can do. Do not read this Scripture and go back to trying.

"If I don't try, I'll fall."

If you do try, you'll fall.

A multitude of groups today are out there teaching the secret way to the "deeper life," and seekers flock to them by the thousands. Those ways don't work. This is true, and it works, but people aren't flocking to it—because they don't want to walk in the light. They want a quick fix that doesn't require so much cleaning of their hearts. They would rather try, or they would rather have a periodic cleansing.

Christians today do not walk in complete joy, nor are they whiter than snow. They are living subnormal Christian lives. However, it is possible to walk in the light as He is in the light. That way, you do not have to get rid of the sins discussed in the previous chapters, because you will not commit them.

I used to be a "tryer" and a charger, and the Lord spared me. I am "doing" more with less effort now than I used to do with effort. This is so contrary to our normal mode of thinking that it may not make sense to you. Ask God to help it make sense so that you can reject trying and trust Him.[21] Books that have helped me walk in the light include *The Calvary Road*, *We Would See Jesus*, and *Broken People, Transforming Grace: The Gospel's Message of Saving Love* by Roy Hession and *Continuous Revival* by Norman Grubb.

21. For more on living by grace through faith, read my book *Dead and Alive: Obedience and the New Man*, available at Amazon.com and ccmbooks.org.

How to Be Free from Any Sin

T he way to be free from any particular kind of sin is to be confessed up to date on every other sin. Why? Sins do not travel in singles. If you want to be free from stealing, be sure you have confessed all your coveting and lying. Victory over single sins is easy when you have been forgiven for all the others. I have addressed different kinds of sins one at a time in this book. However, you need to realize that your sins tend to act together.

Getting rid of these sins will mean confessing and, with that confession, forsaking the sin. Forsaking is not the same as promising not to do it again. It is an *act* of not doing it again. Don't promise not to do it again. When you make a promise like this, you are putting the burden of keeping the promise on yourself. Then when you sin, you sin twice: once because you sinned, and once because you broke your promise. Forsake your sin by turning to God and walking in the light. Turning to Him will turn you away from the sin. Confess your sin now and forsake it now.

> Now to Him who is able to keep you from stumbling,
> And to present you faultless
> Before the presence of His glory with exceeding joy,
> To God our Savior,
> Who alone is wise,
> Be glory and majesty,
> Dominion and power,
> Both now and forever.
> Amen. (Jude 24–25, NKJV)

About the Authors

Jim Wilson has been a pastor and evangelist in Moscow, Idaho, for over forty years. He previously served as an officer in the U.S. Navy and a staff member for Officers' Christian Fellowship.

Bessie Dodds Wilson received Christ at the age of 15 and dedicated her life to Christian ministry. After attending Prairie Bible Institute, she ministered in Alberta homestead country and taught for Inter-School Christian Fellowship. In 1948, she joined the Women's Union Missionary Society as principal of the Kyoritsa Bible School for Women in post-war Yokohama, Japan.

Jim and Bessie met in Japan and married there in 1952. Bessie went to be with her Lord in 2010. Together they raised four children. Their fifteen grandchildren and thirty-four great-grandchildren (and counting) continue to be blessed by their legacy.